How to Beat a Ninja

A Guide for Preparing Oneself for the Inevitable Encounter
with the Ultimate Enemy and Facing Him in Mortal
Combat

By
Dr. Wu Song

Cover and Back design by Germancreative

ISBN 978-0-9600667-0-4

This book is dedicated to Lao Tzu, the first "Ninja" from whom all the arts are descended from...

Introduction

忍者- Ninja

Shinobi. Monomi. Nokizaru. Iga-mono. In Mandarin
Chinese they are "Ren Ze." The very concept itself is a
timeless hyperbole for the impossible that breaks through
every language and cultural barrier. The essence of Ninja is
the dark *Dao*, and he is the very picture of perfection for
the innovators of society, whose path is ultimately neither
acceptable in the warrior nor the scholarly Dao. What
cannot be achieved by brute force or bureaucratic orders, it
shall be through law-breaking and vigilance.

    If Lao Tzu's Dao or "way" can be summarized with
the word "respect," perhaps the Shinobi can settle for
"discretion." Yet, in historically trying to remain unknown
and unseen the Ninja has been popularized to become *the*
icon, the sought-image and goal for legions of aspiring
shadow stalkers in an ironic twist, to the chagrin of their
clan's creed and the generations of Lords they obeyed.
Throughout its many pop cultural mutations, it has been
interpreted in various ways ranging from the supernatural
to the ridiculous. Many modern day "ninjutsu practitioners"
— no doubt on some level of awareness and self-
consciousness of its potential for parody— have the
nagging feeling in the back of their mind that "if he can be
seen, he is not a ninja." Quite correct. Quite frankly, to
practice the art of Ninja is not to train a specific fighting set
or hand-to-hand combat so much as it is in antiquated
methods of espionage and guerilla warfare.

At the time of this writing Jinichi Kawakami is allegedly Japan's last living ninja. Judging from the skills he performed for national television, mostly contortionist-like *taijutsu* and accurate shuriken throwing, he is the closest candidate to satisfying the historical definition of a ninja. Now, Kawakami sensei has declared no heirs to his art. Upon his passing, the historical and original, empirical definition of the ninja art will disappear from the face of the planet forever. You and your descendants will most certainly never encounter any assailant from the Kawakami-san school of ninjutsu in the generations availing the printing of this book, so why bother preparing for an enemy that, in every sense of the word, will finally completely vanish from reality?

The very *notion* of Ninja existing means that the world is imbalanced. Whether or not their origins or roles can actually be ascertained, what does is it say about a society (on both hemispheres!) that admires and glorifies feudal terrorists and exotic assassins? As the canonical Daoist text tells us, the Dao has left Heaven. Yet, as Daoism tells us, as do most of the great philosophies of the world do: rather than trying to change the world, you must change yourself.

How to Use This Book

You bought this book aware that the purchasing of a title does not equate to the learning of its contents. The contents do not boast of any make-believe promises that will be fulfilled upon rereading the book the second, or seventh time. This book does not claim to teach you mystical arts or fantasies because it admits forefront that there are no such things.

Write notes, highlight and mark where you see fit. Most importantly, you must constantly be thinking about how to apply each lesson to a metaphor for the modern life. Readers may use the text as a checklist for self-improvement. If you have a physical copy, you might keep it tucked away in a secretive corner in your room or basement for reference. This book is about Ninja, a being who you may choose to believe exists or not. Some will wrongfully use the contents as a guideline to becoming what their idea of a Ninja is themselves. Those who do not, will use the Ninja as a metaphor for his personal nemesis. After all, if we prepare ourselves to face the ultimate enemy, what have we to fear the lesser ones in life?

This book is split into five parts, three of which can immediately be applied to oneself in their quest for self-perfection and fortitude against Ninja. "Mind" concerns affairs governing intel and the accumulation of wisdom, "Body" contains passages on areas to improve on for physical encounters, and "Soul" concerns the Ninja's distinguishing paradigms. "The Ninja" section is a collection of essays to remind you of the kind of opponent you will be theoretically preparing for and his hypothetical background, providing motivation as well as an eye-opener to the uninitiated. The "Psychology" section concerns the more esoteric part of the book and contains what most trite, cheap "ninjutsu" books offer in generic advice regarding positive thinking and remaining low-key.

Knowing Thyself

Why did Sun Tzu claim, "Know the enemy and know yourself and you need not fear the result of a hundred battles?" It is usually the haughty and loud-mouthed who are eager to accept fights they cannot win, but the tragedy lies in the manner that they were unaware that they would lose before even accepting— After all, the Art of War also reminds us to only enter battles we are certain to win. Because a hefty portion of war-making involves intelligence-gathering, that is exactly what you are encouraged to do in this chapter. You ought to recognize and therefore *work*, striving endlessly to mitigate any weaknesses you have. One should not regard it as an onerous chore or one-time task. To gather and compare information is a way of life, but it should not become an overstressed priority. For example, if you find yourself devoting too much time to book-reading and studying, you are venturing into the scholar territory. You must begin habitually honing a keen eye for bits of knowledge as the merchant covets pennies on roadsides and corners. Think of it as gathering mental ammo for a last stand.

We may begin with the simplest and basest of gathering intel on ourselves. Through the usage our five senses, we shall evaluate the physicality of our corporeal bodies. For starters, you can recognize the body type you have, and incorporating a combat style that suits it. A long, lanky build is not as suited to in-fighting or wrestling as a bulky, shorter frame. A heavy, chiseled physique is not suited for silence and sneaking about. Some Ninja clans had a strict weight limit for recruitment and deployment (for example, no unit may exceed a weight of 58 kilograms, or 130 lbs). Work endlessly to sculpt/cultivate/train the body you desire for the situation— avoid a bulky Adonis-like body that would make you stand out.

To know yourself is to examine your own calligraphy, the faults in the brush strokes and thickness of pressure applied all betray aspects of one's personality. You must acknowledge your personal weaknesses. The over-confident unsurprisingly have the greatest difficulty in identifying areas that they lack in. Bad habits and lifestyle, ego, and health are all subject to scrutiny. Understand how a chronic illness may debilitate you in the moment of urgency or grave importance. Step back and see how you can improve your health starting from the digestive system. Swallow the fact that you do not possess the fastest metabolism among your friend circle and research the best diet for you. If your hygiene and sanitary habits are not to blame for your constant returning cold, it can be due to an ignorance of Yin and Yang chi's relationship within the body. If you fear drowning, you must learn how to swim as soon as possible. If you are unable to recognize your faults from sparring, then have a trusted, more learned friend spot them out and explain them to you.

The psychologist Thomas Stampfl created the concept of *flooding* in 1967, defined as exposing the patient to fear repeatedly in an attempt to desensitize or "ground" them to the particular anxiety, phobia or even posttraumatic stress order. Do you have a fear of heights? This is a severe problem, and should not be confused with the fear of falling of which most of the population is afflicted with. Phobias need to be recognized and dealt with, for rest assured a Ninja will recognize and exploit your idiosyncrasies and defects as any skilled tactician would in discovering holes in the formation of an opposing army's vanguard. Start small, from climbing trees to staring over balconies, to reasonable acts of daring while constantly reminding yourself that once the wave of vertigo is over, that by the end of tonight you will be safely asleep in bed again. It is, after all— to a certain extent— all in your mind. In keeping this mindset for the Ninja, it is absolutely vital that any phobia of the dark be banished. See "Darkness is his Home" under PART 4- The Ninja.

This extends not to just athletic or bodily performance but character and conduct as well, though that arguably is the hardest of all. Pride is a wall that is unfairly strong. Do you find it difficult to apologize and acknowledge wrongdoing? To become a better, more moral person as well as a wise one is the goal of scholars, who yearn to achieve sagehood. However, there are plenty of books depicting and elucidating upon this process in detail, and it is beyond the scope that this book covers. Understand that overall, you need to already possess a personality that does not make it likely for you to earn enemies.

Misinformed laymen misunderstand the accumulation of intelligence, confusing it for passive hoarding of knowledge. Practical intel-gathering in militaries most often stems from a question. However, this "passive hoarding" is exactly what you should be doing, even if you are not immediately determining how to face the Ninja threat.

Know the Environment

Be it steppe, a deciduous forest, a night market or the inner cities, you shall know your surroundings. Do you know the local edible plants and insects? Can you identify edible or poisonous fungi? Do you know which streets in the neighborhood are safe or frequented by gangs? The terrain dictates what footwork is limited for combat or speed of locomotion. For example, in a forest, one ought to move slowly to remain undetected, due to numerous bramble and natural impediments on the ground which may alert if disturbed, or leave an easily traceable trail. Ninjas are required to have thorough knowledge and awareness of their environment. They utilized ancient, albeit somewhat superstitious and unreliable knowledge to interpret tell-tale signs of incoming rain (heavy precipitation muffled their sneaking). Loud cicadas would somewhat cloak the crunching of fallen leaves; the roar of a nearby river or waterfall would achieve the same effect as heavy traffic or a noise-polluted city.

Before stepping foot outside, you should know the weather. The brightness and hour of the sun can be implemented during the minute of combat by positioning yourself with the back against it and the enemy's eyes towards the glare of the rays. Be conscious of not just the natural climate, but also the culture. Be aware of current trends, cultures and taboos. Notice how bustling the streets tend to be, what is acceptable in matters pertaining to public conduct and in contrast, what is considered facetious, etc. Be aware of how your dialect/slang/lingo will contrast with or make you stand out among the locale. For practice, see if your knowledge is sufficient enough to pinpoint tourists or clear outsiders to the region.

Observation is a treasure. Always look before you make the leap. If you were unable to scout the obstacle course or rooftops beforehand, your eye should develop a skill for judging the sturdiness of the material you are about to land or climb upon. You should also hone an immediate sense of your environment on a macro level. As you tread the streets, your mind is mapping multiple, alternative paths to your destination, as well as remembering landmarks and salient buildings to identify your location to others. Smell changes in the air and any unusual, alarmingly strong odors. Listen to commotions or outbursts indicating possible danger. Pay special attention to avenues of escape, such as a convenient alley, a sewer, an abandoned construction building, etc. Attempt to be alert in the current situation rather than letting your mind drift to stress-inducing tasks yet to be complete or things that have occurred in the past. Do not traverse the city absent or cloudy-minded. If you have a bad sense of direction, this needs to be rectified immediately.

Because you are avoiding being noticeable or obvious, unusual occurrences or abnormalities should immediately stick out to you. Compare the timeliness of things. Speculate on the congestion of traffic or a delayed performance. Notice the members who are tardy to the meeting. Question the volume of things, both audio and metaphorical. Could the rather loud attraction or incident in a city function as a distraction? Obviously, this must be applied to human individuals. Clothes and appearances are easy to arrest your attention. Regard the fellow making a fool of himself at a safe distance. Eye the man with the deathly pale pallor with caution. Realize the amateur operative trying his hardest to appear normal but adversely singling himself even more.

In interiors such as a conference room or other enclosed spaces like alleys, switch paradigms if need be. Those high in emotional intelligence can read the mood and take their leave depending on how foreboding and hostile the aura of the room seems- in other words, they can sense a fight or conflict about to spark. It is not your job to diffuse the situation- that is a duty of the virtuous scholar's or the noble warrior's aspirations. You shall not interfere in the business of others, nor dabble in another person's problem. If blood or chaos is a possibility, it is your responsibility to look after yourself and exit yourself from the equation (See "Escape" under PART 2- Body).

Acquisition of Skills

"The ancient masters must be studied constantly without respite, even when the practitioner thinks he has grasped knowledge."
-Miyamoto Musashi, *Book of Five Rings*

Seek information that would give you a slight edge over your fellow average man. Learn alternate forms of communication or codes, from ciphers, Morse, Braille, sign language, etc. Take up skills which in this day and age may be accessible to anyone with the wherewithal and time to learn, such as rock-climbing or martial arts. Buy a lock-picking set and learn how to navigate by the stars.

Do not dismiss seemingly outdated knowledge or skills. What if your city happened to fall within the vicinity of an EMP's influence? Can you compete with the feudal warrior's versatility, his ruggedness and survival competence? Can you start a fire without a lighter? Can you ride a horse? Depending on which hemisphere you are operating in, you may read that region's classics in order to form an adequate understanding for that society's development of values and how it has evolved. Ideally, we would have enough time to expand our research to all corners of the world, but time is precious. Discern good titles from redundant or mundane ones, asking thyself the reason and relevance for reading each volume. Look into literature as a mirror, as a reflection of the human condition. Make productive usage and application of your time. Collecting information and feeding fantasies without discerning fact from fiction is masturbatory, unproductive and self-defeating.

Exercise:
Edward de Bono promulgated the term "Lateral Thinking" in 1967, citing the earliest example as the biblical judgment of Solomon, in his wise ability to determine which woman was the true mother of the disputed infant. It is essentially solving questions that do not have obvious answers from creative deduction. A Ninja would have no trouble solving Lateral Thinking puzzles. Try one right now:

She died because she packed too quickly. How did she die?

Answer: She was a sky diver who packed her parachute too quickly. It did not deploy correctly when she pulled the ripcord

Knowing the Enemy

In a sense, this book is one great Daoist mental exercise on the perfect enemy. Buddhists meditate on impossibilities by asking themselves questions such as "what does the sound of one hand clapping sound like?" A common question and introduction to students in epistemology is to ask if it is possible to "truly know" anyone else. Do you really know your lover or the individual members of your own family? Does living and being physically or platonically intimate with someone mean you know the true motivations and innermost thoughts of their heart? The desires of individuals differ, interact, conflict and rub off on each other as inevitably as hydrogen and oxygen molecules. The most humble of couples do not let voice their most perturbed thoughts, and for the greater good. Even kin brothers have things to hide from their siblings. Civilizations have survived on the restraint of the tongue and the burial of secrets. To let others know of our true judgments of others; our true desires and perversions, our secrets, is to give our vulnerabilities to them. The more you talk and reveal yourself like an audio journal to the recipient, the more predictable you become to them.

Stretched to its limits, one who can know his enemy to the closest 99.99 percentile knows every hair on the enemy's body. He knows the date and what sign his enemy was born under. He knows the lodge, orphanage or homes the enemy has grown up in. He can distinguish between the enemy's identical twins. He knows the enemy's friends and family as well as his own. He knows and has contact with the enemy's enemies. He knows the enemy's schedule like the back of his hand. He knows which temples, establishments, parks or dens the enemy frequents or would go to for sanctuary. He knows the enemy's employer, what vehicle he uses to travel, and his place of residence. He knows the enemy's finances as well as any alternative forms of income and currency he may be keeping secret. He knows all of the enemy's personas and can imitate his lingo and rhetoric for each one. He knows the enemy's languages and can comprehend and speak them all fluently. He can tell when the enemy is telling a truth, or a lie. He notices the volatility of the enemy's decision-making or the stability of his all around conduct. He will be able to predict every tactical move the enemy makes and have the foresight to see the blunders before they occur. He knows his enemy's level of allegiance to his nation, group, or people. He will know the enemy's current standing in politics and religion, and he will know what makes him tick accordingly. He knows the enemy's values, what Gods he worshipped, present and past, and his level of devotion. He knows the enemy's superstitions, his deepest fears, fetishes, regrets and guilt. He knows the enemy's favorite foods, as well as the foods he cannot or will not eat. He knows every disease harboring in the enemy's body and what would aggravate or cure them. He knows which teachers the enemy has called "master," and the current mentor he serves now. He knows what style the enemy fights with. He knows the enemy's training routine and his techniques ahead of time. He knows the enemy's timing and accuracy, his balance or lack of it. Come actual combat, he will predict without error every step the enemy will take, the angle of his next strike, and the reaction he will give from a response. He will not be surprised if his enemy deviates or acts erratically from his normal behavior, because he has taken into account every possible aberration and the probability of them occurring as well. He knows the efforts and level of preparation the enemy invested into traps and defenses, and will detect them before even seeing them. He knows the one person, being, or object the enemy cherishes above all others and the lengths he will go to save him, her or it. He knows the enemy at his highest, and he knows the enemy at his lowest. He knows exactly how his enemy acts before death, from his last words to his reaction, be it a chilly repose or wretched begging. He knows the enemy's place in this world, in every sense of the phrase. He knows at this very moment where the enemy is and what he is doing. This is what the Ninja knows about you.

Knowledge of the enemy is not just leverage to use against the enemy (i.e. blackmail). Limiting the use of spies and bugs just for confrontation, extortion or humiliation is superficial thinking. The primary goal of gathering information of the enemy, and arguably all Daoist learning- is *prediction*. And that is what those idiotic ninjutsu books fail to actually teach you. It is about being able to predict patterns of existence, without empirical evidence. It is an art, and not a science. The more we know about a person, the more we tend to be able to guess correctly their next move or course of action. Understandably, this can change and turn out to be wildly different to our predictions due to gaps in our knowledge. To be able to predict is therefore *power*, and to become erratic and defiant of categorization and equations is to fight against it.

Tui Bei Tu

Its name roughly translated in Chinese means, "Push Back Picture-" a mysterious document that was possibly written during the 7th century Tang Dynasty in China. The authors Li Chunfeng and Yuan Tiangang used their profound understanding of metaphysics and the Way (道) with Daoist numerology to divine images telling of events in the future. There are a total of sixty illustrations, each one surreal and astoundingly difficult to interpret; all are accompanied by an equally cryptic poem. Devotees and aficionados are unable to reach consensus upon which of the pictures represents humanity's current state, the most popular opinions being that of the three pictures above which are said to either summarize the Chinese civil war or the advent of the third World War.

Keep track of current events while learning to remain skeptical and discerning fake and real journalism. Do not get too caught up in news that is irrelevant, distracting and has little to nothing to do with you, and of which you have no power to alter or better. Understand that scientific research is driven by economics. Culture and economics feed into each other as do being and non-being. The answers you seek in the quest for the truth may be distorted or simply not there because of the lack of incentive or conflicting business interests to uncover them.

Read and attain a solid understanding of basic psychology. Learn generic signs of body language, as well as how to maintain thy own facial language. One way to view accessories or makeup is to view them as distractions. Why would Aphrodite ruin her physiognomy with hoop earrings?

- *Fingertips touching together in a mounted, pyramid-like angle indicates a feeling of superiority in the individual.*

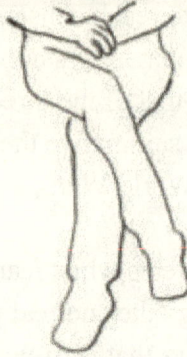

- *Legs tightly crossed indicate a social barrier or openness to addressee.*

- *Be able to sense the tensing of certain muscles, such as the shoulders or waist. Good martial artists are able to detect and point out instantly where a muscle is underperforming in a beginner during a particular movement or pose. Those skilled at reading people will also be able to sense areas of anxiety and insecurity in individuals during a conversation or greeting.*

- *Notice "tics" in the face during the split-second they occur, right before the individual fixes them. Be wary of your own "tics," especially if you employ a stoic exterior frequently.*

Learn emotional cues and the proper time to speak, which 95% of the time will be, "never." File information about people in your head, if it may just be assumptions based on their appearances. You shall research the operative, if you are able to identify him. Employ every trick of the trade, because he WILL use them against you.

Pay attention to the breathing of the subject. Does it demonstrate mastery of chi usage, or is the person's breath shallow and never reaches below his lungs? What does this say about the current mental disposition of the subject? If you focus your ears, does the subject produce a sickly wheeze or an animated cough? Heavy-breathing could indicate signs of exertion or a physical weakness which can easily be exploited. True silence in breathing is the apex of its art. Very few people in this modern world exhale the breath of tranquillity through their lungs, and fewer know

how to use the *dan tian*, the conceptual lower cavity under
their belly button in Chinese medicine.

*A belt is wrapped securely around the upper thoracic
cavity to encourage breathing deeper beyond the lungs into
the deeper recesses of the torso, specifically the lower
region of the 丹田 "dan tian."*

*Basic standing chi gong drill- Stand feet slightly shoulder
width apart, then raise hands using "chi" to inflate the
arms rather than forcing with stiff motor movement until
they are above the head. Imagine this to be the beginning of
a "chi shower," and that the air you breathe in is washing
the internal organs you glide over with your hands. Slowly
lower arms until they are in front of the chest, palms
inward facing the chest. Then lower the arms until they are
at waist level, palms still facing inward. Finish by bringing
hands together, resting on the abdomen. You can repeat*

this motion several times. Upon completion, breathe in multiples of 9, 36 being a safe number according to Daoist principles.

Recognize how your body posture appears in public and adopt a more suitable one for the environment and situation. Your overall goal is to achieve elusiveness, and sometimes this amounts to appearing mundane or even displaying meekness. The Taichi or Wu Dang-originated arts of China teach the practitioner to render his entire body structure soft. When done correctly it can be done at will, maintained in public, even while walking. One interpretation of Taichi is that it is the physical compromise of Daoist and Confucian principles, and one glance at the relaxed Taichi posture certainly evokes ideas of submission, a virtue in antiquated Chinese culture. Compare this ideal body posture in contrast to the preferred dominant, confident Western pose.

- *Spine is deceptively straight; the lower lumbar aligned whereas the natural spine would remain in a "S" shape. This is achieved by tilting the groin*

slightly forward. With the shoulders relaxed completely forward out of their sockets, it looks almost as if the practitioner is hunching. In the cellular level, his muscles and ligaments have become yielding and as malleable as water, meaning that a strike can be achieved within seconds.

- *The confident, open posture of the Western man desires to speak aloofness to being challenged, and he had best be able to prove it through might what he conveys through swagger.*

It would be extremely helpful to be able to identify the rank of your Ninja. It is unlikely that you would be given any salient giveaways such as the color of belt he is wearing (and even then, there lies the difficulty in affirming whether their color-coding system is universal or not), but information like this once procured becomes valuable and potentially life-saving. A generic ranking of Ninja are as follows: If he is a *Genin*, meaning a fresh beginner who still has yet to gone under his rites of passages, assess the threat as you would of an expert assassin. A *Chonin* is experienced and even more deadly. *Jonin* are highly dangerous because they resemble generals given a license by their lords to kill and judge as they see fit, and thus tactics and plans will have to be adjusted accordingly.

PART 2— Body

Conditioning

Diet

You may not train every day, but you *may* eat every day. The corporeal body can be fed a constant but reliable source of fuel in order to function, but calories and nutrients are not uniform. Avoid foods which rot the teeth or foul the breath, as well as foods that impart very little yield in energy. The food you eat should not leave you feeling sluggish or dull.

There are varying accounts on the ninja diet. Every family had their own recipe for super foods allegedly allowing them to sustain on very little. Some families, especially during the dominance of Buddhism in Japan, limited themselves to strictly vegetarian diets. These vegetarian diets were thought to cleanse the body and spirit of maladies, odors and other unwanted symptoms that would betray the Ninja's mission, and consisted of glorified trail mixes and bean curds.

Feel free to experiment, from an all seafood diet (sushi and sashimi) to that of carb-heavy buns. Some Ninja clans' recipes for buns had fillings of various different seeds and other "super foods" for nutrition. If there is a goal you must immediately develop, it is insensitivity and impartiality of the sense of taste. Are there any foods you are averse to, for the mere reason of disagreeing with your palate? Brace yourself and dull your tongue to the texture and flavor. However repulsive a food may seem, at least it is not medicine, or worse— poison. You can train yourself to not taste or smell the food you eat, which requires much spirit or even trauma to occur. Immediate practice can begin with familiarizing oneself with dried, preserved foods and military rations.

Temperance is a discipline in itself. Becoming a glutton and possessing an abnormally demanding appetite requires and wastes provisions. Slow down the body's metabolism. This may be achieved through eating larger meals and less frequently, as well as fasting and meditation. Make the most out of less. Abstain from alcohol or other harmful, useless carbohydrates. Educate yourself on nutrients.

Flexibility/Stretching/Calisthenics

Flexibility is a vital skill in combat and the art of stealth. Contortionism in addition to explosive speed is an essence of Eastern martial arts. You should be able to kick an opponent of your height in the temple, while maintaining the leg outstretched at that height. Every muscle fiber should be contributing to the strain and effort of raising a limb. If you are unable to do dynamic stretching, a warm shower or a soft, internal skill such as Chinese chi gong can increase the body's yang energy in order to safely warm up the muscles, joints and ligaments before a stretch.

Your back and core strength must be strong, yet flexible. You should be able to do a bridge, which enables you to arch your back and transition into other movements. You should be able to touch the elbows together, squeezing the pectoral muscles while doing so. You should be able to reach hands behind to clasp fingers and navigate the wrists in the dreaded scenario that they are tied together. You should be able to do a split. You should be able to squeeze through nooks and crannies where normal humans find it difficult to pass their body into or through. You should be less susceptible to certain joint locks or body manipulations due to your flexibility. Those who are triple-jointed will revel in their talent. The majority who are not will have to train, day and night. If the ligaments and muscles have been fine-tuned to the cellular level you would move lithely as a cat, the relaxation of your body like water.

You should be able to walk on your toes for long periods of time, completely silent. You should be able to snap into and maintain horse stance for long periods of time. You should be able to adapt and alter your current movement in the advent of incoming barriers or detection. You should be able to freeze during any position of your movement and remain completely still and lifeless, devoid of vibration and heartbeat.

The training and refining of one's body is not accomplished with aesthetics as a priority, unless disguise and spy work is of concern. Large, cumbersome equipment is not necessary for the Ninja's conditioning and strength training. Everything he needs, he already possesses. Thus he has done more one-handed pushups than there are stars in the night sky. Because he has familiarized himself with countless exercises of his own body-weight through endless repetition, he is aware of the limits of his physical body, while also having transcended the capabilities of normal men.

You are not limited to the absence of a particular training tool, for your own gravity and limits are all you require. You can focus on certain isometrics, targeting specific muscles of the body even while casually walking or in moments of sedentary rest. You can add plyometric elements to your workouts, training the explosiveness of muscle fibers as well as the nerves. Everything from the most basic push-up to neck exercises in order to brace the head for a punch should be trained with the question of function in mind: what does this workout target and/or serve?

The burpee's primary function in boxing training is to train the body to become alert and snapped to attention upon rising from the floor.

You should be able to do a muscle-up. You should be able to sink to the floor using only one leg without injuring the knee. You should be able to meditate for long periods of time in the lotus position. You should be able to climb and hang using only your fingertips and toes. You should be able to hang from tall places like a sloth, with only your arms, not tiring. You should be able to walk on your hands. You should be able to run a long distance without tiring. You should be able to lift something twice your own body weight.

Body Hardening

Depending on the exact kind of conditioning and the level of exertion, you can practice toughening the bones of the body anywhere. Sharpen elbows by lightly chipping away at walls, posts, or trees. Certain schools of Karate condition the strength of the shoulders while hardening the knuckles. Okinawan Karate popularized the idea of punching a wooden striking post known as a makiwara. Several old, bare knuckle boxing techniques from England implemented crude methods to harden the knuckles. Shaolin martial arts frequently abuse the practitioners' flesh to prove Buddhist principles stressing the intransigence of the corporeal as well as the all-too-real sensation of pain, or suffering. Some South-Asian martial arts utilize partner drills where opposing partners clash each other's forearms and other limbs in unison in order to harden them. Many, many martial arts teach themselves to regard the most ubiquitous and hardest objects in nature as punching bags: from rocks, a mountain wall, to trees, of the soft and hardwood variety. Muay Thai is infamous for its traditional training of kicks by hardening the shins on young banana trees. Some Silat fighters break open coconuts and kick hardwood trees full speed.

Many of these martial arts which implement esoteric breathing techniques into their training derive their influence from Chinese origins. The controlled breathing serves many functions from drawing power from the chi reservoir (known as the *dan tian*) in order to deliver a supernaturally powerful blow to hardening the body. A misconception is that such displays of weapon-breaking against flesh are primarily for combat, but arguably this is more effective for the mind. It would be difficult to replicate the same cellular process under stress and adrenaline. Rather, if one has been conditioned to not fear the edge of a spear on one's throat, the fear of the weapon will wane as well as fear of defeat. Knowing — or expecting — victory is half the battle. There exists plenty of documents and video media illustrating the triumph of man's effort and will over his weapons and tools, which since Neolithic times gave him the fangs and claws that he lacked against beasts.

Body-hardening, despite its name, can be as something as simple as desensitizing one's skin to pain (such as repeatedly battering one's torso with a rattan stick or rolling the shins with a metal bar). There also exists the more extreme feats of body-hardening, which can be likened to exhibitions. The very mortal fear of falling is countered by jumping from extreme heights in some martial arts. Some Wu Dang martial artists jump from heights of four, even five meters and land on the earth with a solid planting on both feet, without breaking the fall or bending the knees, in an attempt to demonstrate the strength of their chi. Temporarily walking across a surface lit on fire or heated coals, crawling on broken glass and other sharp objects is done in everything from ancient martial arts initiation to modern military training. Be sure to seek legitimate instructors who train properly and intelligently. Be wary of ignorant instructors who unwittingly do irrevocable damage to their students' nervous systems and internal organs in "conditioning" their heads and bodies for punches, or demanding absurd sacrifices to their physical well-being to prove loyalty.

Combat

You do not have wings. Hence, your being on the ground makes you feel vulnerable. Conversely this makes the Ninja confident. Once he dives to snatch you in his talons as a bird of prey, you will turn on him with such ferocity that you will clip his wings. Show by action that his target was not the defenseless hare on the plain, but a furious honey badger or wolverine. Give him the fight of his life. Be aware that no training in a book may substitute for actual combat training. Do not pursue a ninja alone, even in the seemingly most optimal of lighting and conditions. A Ninja may use a similar tactic used by all the nomadic steppe tribes North of China long before it was a conglomeration of dynasties: feigning a retreat and then annihilating the pursuers in a shower of arrows once they have taken the bait, or they can drop caltrop strips to injure the feet.

A general rule of thumb encourages you to be cautious of using jumping or spinning attacks, the former making you unable to change direction while airborne, and the latter exposing your back momentarily to the enemy, despite the Ninja's fondness of using these types of moves himself. Always train proper timing, coordination and power using the appropriate tools and mentality. Aim to achieve speed faster than the average student, for when fighting a Ninja it seems as if every motion and time itself is on fast-forward. Theoretically, if a student has only an endless supply of fighters and volunteers to spar and train with, he would still need the tools appropriate to his art to train *isolated* skills. Explore and experiment. Cross-train with boxing speed bags, Muay Thai "banana" bags, Chinese kung fu "wooden dummies," etc. Do not forget to rely on nature as your ancestors did. Punch falling leaves from trees. Splash water from a clean river or stream into your eyes to force them to remain open in the blur and rage of combat (make sure the water is clean- you must protect your eyes).

In regards to "seeing" a Ninja: If the mainstream joke postulates that Ninja are impossible to detect or simply even to catch a glimpse of, then there is actually no reason you should not take this epigram to heart (see "Darkness is His Home" under PART 4- Ninja). Especially when the dreaded moment presents itself in combat— the Ninja will prove to live up to every myth and parody to his name, and be no more than a blur even in visible daylight. Preserve your senses and sensibility at all costs, and train accuracy at night whether it be practicing shooting or close quarters fighting. This is why you are encouraged to spot differences, whether it be in isolated activities such as puzzles or in the vagaries of fellow men (see "Daily Conduct" under Part 3- Soul).

Theory

You should study while remaining critical of other martial arts' terminology such as "centerline," ranging concepts such as "largo" or "close range" in fencing or kali, etc. (This would fall under the subcategory of "Know your Enemy" under "Mind." Learning to separate imagination, myth and assumption from physics and reality can still only empower you only so much).

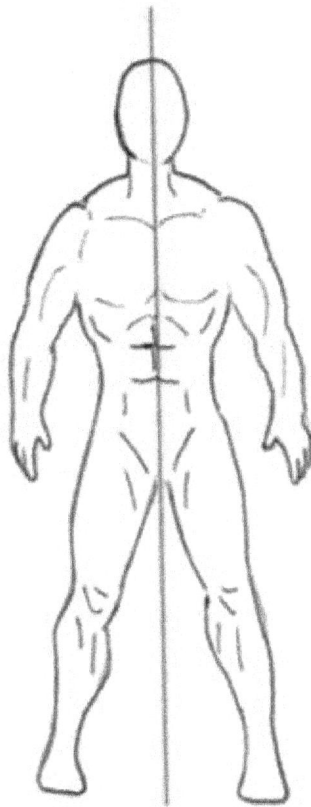

- *The "centerline," the theoretical vertical axis driving through the subject's center of gravity*

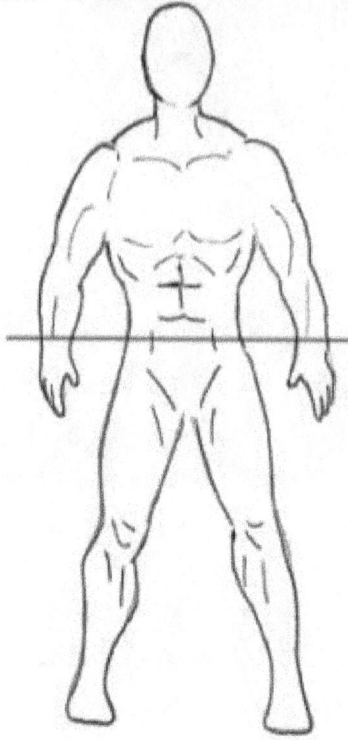

- *The "middle/low line," the theoretical "latitude" of the body of which everything above it is susceptible to striking, and everything below targeted for takedowns/low kicks.*
- *Close range/middle range/long range in both Western Olympic fencing and Doce Pares Eskrima. Some schools of weapon martial arts disregard concepts of ranges entirely, such as Pekiti Tirsia Kali believing that two fighters within "no man's land" means mutual destruction.*

Familiarize yourself with combat sport lexicon, while also taking time to uncovering its older and more ancient ancestors. Understand the basis for these theories while also questioning and forming alternatives to countering their solutions. Study angles of attack, and the optimal footwork required in order to place oneself in an advantageous position while positioning the enemy in a fatal one.

If you should develop a healthy interest in the dead Occidental weapon arts, such as Spanish circles for fencing, or medieval tactics for brawling in armor, take care to avoid falling victim to vapid recreation or lies. Form a mental cladogram of a martial art, becoming aware of its original founders, detractors, what traits it inherited and lost as it evolved, and so on. Know the objective, historical facts detailing which art beat which, and be superior to blind loyalty or nationalism behind a culture's art. Deny falsehood and take note where an art has borrowed/stolen from another. Do not defend your practiced martial arts from ridicule, criticism or scrutiny as if they were your own children— everything is open to questioning. Whatever shortcomings your arts seem to represent, you will work to overcome them through harder training or adopting another style to cover your corners. Do not believe in the false mantra that all martial arts are equal. In a sense, comparing martial arts is ultimately comparing technology- would a blunderbuss compete with an automatic?

Read the biographies of real warriors and men who have made fighting their careers and way of life, as well as secondary sources and complementary texts. Take notes and inspiration from their training routines and of their cultured or humble backgrounds. Understand the mentalities behind the testosterone and blood-scarred exteriors, what enables them to maul like beasts and endure like bulwarks. Miyamoto Musashi's concept of "spirit" as described in *The Book of Five Rings* emphasizes switching between spirits or mentalities such that one would adapt and switch styles to suit combat on the fly. Thus, controlling and projecting your own spirit while reading the opponent's spirit become two different skills on their own. Whether or not one believes in the sixth sense, one must utilize his five sense with maximum efficiency so that he can quickly intake all the signs and giveaways upon his opponent's face/posture in order to accurately read his spirit, and in turn adopt the spirit appropriate for context.

Study video analyses and breakdowns of professional fighters to supplement your brain. Observe their favorite methods; combos; their idiosyncrasies; when they err; how they behave to the press in comparison to how they seem in the ring; their composure or lack of it; the looseness of their muscles and limbs; how they move their feet. Try to see from their point of view during the tension of the first round; figure the inner workings of their mind as you observe them testing and waiting for their opponent to make an error. Do not limit yourself to just the giants— observe amateur or local fights to understand how average fighters or laymen fight. Test in actual sparring with non-cooperating, live partners. Acquire a few simple but reliable combos that you can use again and again with succession. Learn how to set each particular strike, combo, or throw. Learn the counters for each strike or move used against you. Learn the feints for both empty-handed and weapon fighting. Feints are a more advanced but critical component in anyone's arsenal and fighting knowledge.

Familiarize yourself with the concept of rhythm in fighting, which differs depending on weapon and style. The rhythm for a brawl in a street fight is different from boxing, for example.

Obtain an adequate understanding of the human anatomy. Learn vital organs (liver, heart) and vulnerable areas (back of the temple behind the ear) for striking. Learn the locations and names of major arteries and nerves for cutting and slashing. Learn the breakability of bones. Do not limit your targets to what are only viable and legal for sport— aim for kidneys, the spine, and the back of the head, etc.

- *The chin is the most coveted target in combat sports for a reason, possessing many nerve-endings to the brain which if severed shuts the limbic functions off. However, the hardness of the chin must be taken into account so that hands or toes are not injured after impact.*
- *The largest organ to target effectively on the human torso is the liver, with many nerve-endings that make it painful should it be done damage. Take note how a man positions himself with left or right leg either exposes or hides the liver, as the liver rests on the right side of all humans.*
- *Learn the arteries and the detrimental effects should they be cut. The Carotid arteries are not symmetrical and located on the neck. The Radial Ulna may be a common target in a knife duel since they are in the forearms, and the Brachial Artery is located in the upper arm. The Femoral Artery runs*

on the inner side of the legs, and the Aorta is dead center of the torso.

Learn that the groin of men is not necessarily always the Achilles heel it is portrayed to be, and that to attack the eye may not incapacitate a foe with strong will.

BONUS: How a Ninja Fights

Deprived of weapons, tools, or tricks, he would employ head movement that appears supernaturally disjointed, as if he were a whip-like snake or gecko. Footwork is quite unusual, and may or may not be animal-based. Unsurprisingly he relies on speed, and his primary punch is the jab, with abnormally fast retraction. His jab is usually in the form of a finger jab or a blade hand to chop the vulnerable soft targets of the neck and eyes. Any fist or kick he throws will be snapped, though he occasionally finishes with a pushing karate punch. He hides the extent of his abilities early in the fight, but if it drags out longer than expected, he will execute nasty surprises such as a scorpion kick, or outrageous, humanly impossible abilities such as jumping more than two meters high and attacking from an impossible angle.

Scenarios

While it would be impossible to prepare for the perfect ambush set up by a Ninja, what you can do instead is to familiarize yourself with the brutalities of real confrontations. Learn to recognize signs of a storm before it happen. Beware of sucker punches. Recognize patterns in coordinated group attacks. One method of the French Apache gang, whose members dominated the streets of France in the early 20th century, was to ask for the time from a well-dressed, unsuspecting lad. While the gentleman checked his watch, he is pelted in the face with the gang member's hat and then headbutted violently.

This is why situational awareness is so important. Do not be the one to cross a street, especially at night, with ears obscured and attention occupied by your cell phone or portable music player. Become sensitive to common indications of an untrained, aggressive layman about to initiate the first strike. Be conscious of the emotional "flow" of the conversation, when it is verging dangerously high beyond acceptable tensions. A hunched back, widening or narrowed eyes, heavy breathing or holding of breath are common giveaways.

Understand that combat will change based on terrain (see terrain in "Mind,") for example, what if your back was against the wall? How will footwork be limited or change in a slanted elevation, or suboptimal weather? How does restricted lighting or a narrow passageway confine your range of movement and self-defense? See "Know the Environment" under "Mind." One way to view fighting is a physical expression of the entity Chaos. This is the realm of unharmony, randomization and confusion. Several variables will exponentialize the chaos, meaning anything can happen. Variables such as the number of participants, the inclusion of weapons, and more will escalate the chance for absurdity. You may sustain injuries in areas you did not expect to be bruised or cut. You shall not become surprised at the most outlandish deviation from the expected narrative of a duel or fight.

Hand-to-hand

Man has relied on stone and metals to compensate for his lack of fangs and claws since Neolithic times. Relying upon hands should be therefore be a last resort. If by some chance you find yourself unprepared or disarmed, grab a nearby stone, or a solid cylindrical object in your pocket to give more mass and impact to your punch. Be sure to pay attention to protean footwork for any form of combat, both empty-handed and when equipped with weapons. Concern and morality for the enemy comes before and after mortal combat. In the advent of an actual Ninja, you must attack with the intent to kill. Be wary of legal boundaries concerning concealed carry before settling on a kubaton, palmstick, etc.

Make the conscious decision between striking close-knuckled or open-handed. If you have not conditioned or do not already train in a martial art where you harden the bones of the hand, punching with a bare fist can result in broken fingers or wrists. There exist two solutions for this, other than wrapping the hands or using any form of protective gear. A quick and safe alternative is to keep knuckles at a 45 degree diagonal slant. Remember to avoid striking with the thumb or pinky, as these fingers can be easily broken.

Upon impact, the fist lands diagonally upon its target. The diagonal principle allows straight and horizontal hook punches to be safely thrown without compressing the wrist or bruising the knuckles from a vertically-torqued punch.

The other solution is to utilize different methods of striking. The surface areas for impact can take shape in the form of the fingers, blade of the hand, palm, forearm, back knuckles (also called a "back fist"), hammer fist, elbow, shoulder, wrist, knee, and head. Each method should be extensively trained for speed and proper body mechanics, and experimented on a bag or target.

Fingers

Fingers absolutely need to be conditioned, whether through finger push-ups or striking sand and other objects. Be careful to not over-train and start from small steps- begin with a basic plank-holding using all ten fingers slightly apart instead of fully launching into ten reps of two-finger pushups. Be aware that the consequences of traditional finger-conditioning may stunt or truncate the growth of the fingers, whittling each digit to match the same length, for example. Even at their toughest, fingers should not be abused by striking a target as hard as the skull (imagine if they were blocked by forearms or elbows). Targets should include the throat, groin or eyes.

- *Clawing, Flicker jabs or Jeet Kun Do eye jabs, if missed, can be broken from striking a hard surface such as the forehead.*
- *Chinese Leopard fist collapses the fingers which in addition to the throat can also strike the solar plexus or lower belly.*

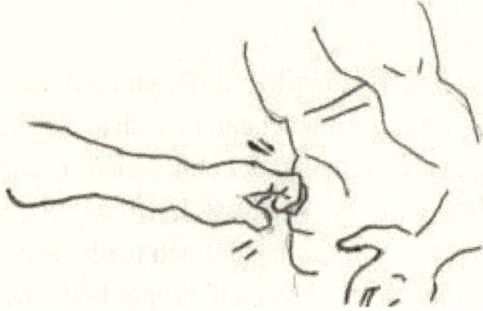

Blade of the Hand

Although a knife hand or karate chop can be swung with the full range of motion of an ax, they ought to be delivered in quick succession from the elbows or utilizing the back muscles in an explosive manner. All the fingers must be tight and not be loose apart, and take care not to accidentally strike with the pinky landing first instead. Target the throat, sides of the neck, the underside of the nose, or the solar plexus.

Palm

You have a wide variety of options with palms, with the motions of pushing or to slap being its exclusive movements. Do differentiate between pushing and punching, as with the former you are not striking to make contact with the target fast enough to conclude the connection with a snap, and are exerting muscle to force the target forward, which you did not do with velocity. Pushing can be done as a way to wreck an opponent's equilibrium to set up for a more devastating punch or elbow, or simply function as a punch in an open-handed method.

You can easily substitute punching with knuckles with the surface of the palms, pushing through like in Kung fu styles or Karate. The optimal point of contact is the lower part of the palm, near where it connects to the wrist. Some Taichi styles tilt the palm diagonally, torquing outwards upon connection for circular energy.

Slapping is a safe alternative to punching. It can be delivered with maximum force and still not injure the hand or wrists, since the energy is evenly distributed across the hand. Because slapping is much safer than shooting fists, you have a wide option of targets.

- *Palm-punching as a substitute to a rear straight punch from boxing.*

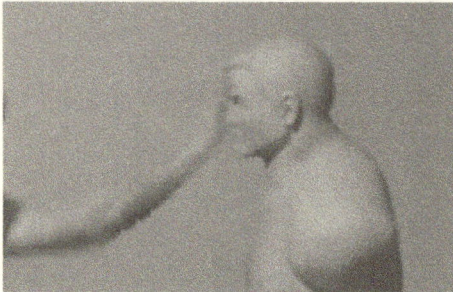

- *Palm-pushing an opponent's chin after intercepting a punch.*

- *Slapping the full frontal area of the face will force tears out of the subject's eyes, momentarily blinding him as well as stunning him. Here it can be used as a lead jab.*

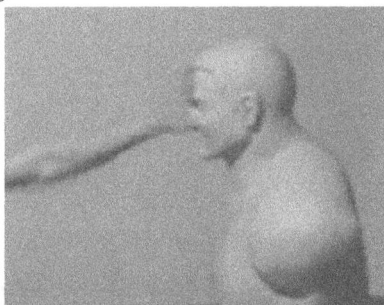

- *The mechanics for a slap to the ear can be exactly substituted for a horizontal hook in boxing. The eardrums may rupture and a slap to the temple or chin may even knock him out.*

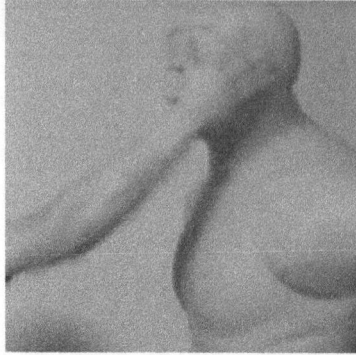

- *If you have your opponent bent over, you can slap forcefully on his kidneys. A transition from attacking the upper body involves controlling the arm then flowing into a slap on one of the sides of the back.*

Forearm

More important in their function for defense, aside from resting as a guard or forcefully parrying and blocking strikes, forearms can be viewed as vertical, stubbier sticks to directly attack as well, albeit very limited in motion; speed and therefore damage. Often times a forearm strike is achieved as an accident or byproduct from another overextended or missed strike, and should be thrown as such. While similar in motion for a blade hand or stick swing, throwing forearm strikes will be considerably slower. Use the bladed edges of the forearm, rather than the fleshy posterior and anterior surfaces (which will be conditioned for blocking).

- *Forearm strike from above against the face.*

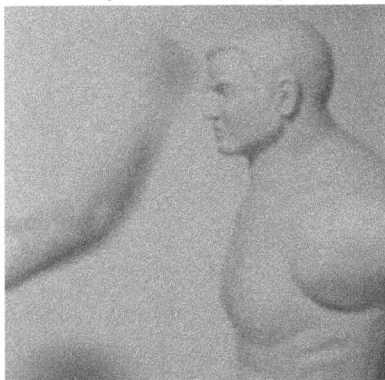

- *Forearm strike against the eyes and bridge of the nose, ideally executed in a whip-like motion. However, in this picture it is used at point-blank range to push and obstruct the target's vision.*

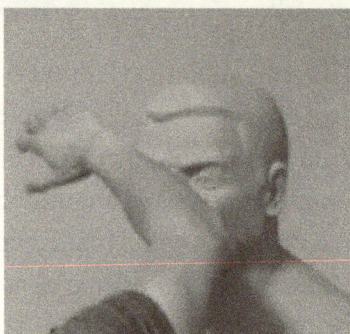

- *Forearm strike down against the torso to destabilize opponent's stance, setting up for a punch or elbow.*

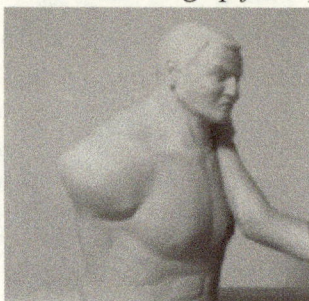

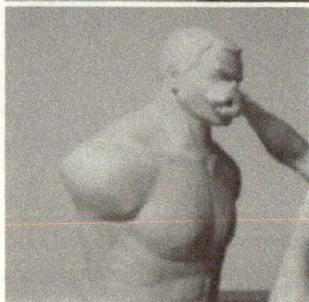

Back fist

Back fists should be executed like an angular jab, reliant on speed rather than power. Because it is essentially a whip-like jab, it needs to be faster on the retract in order to avoid being read, blocked, trapped or cut.

- *Back fist jab into the face*

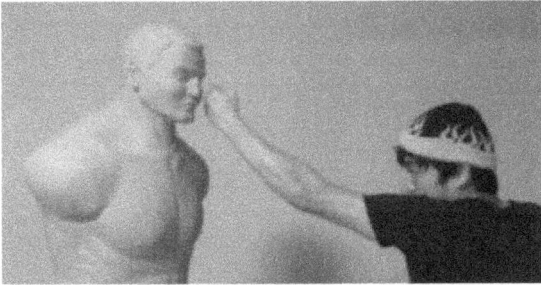

- *Back fist into the solar plexus*

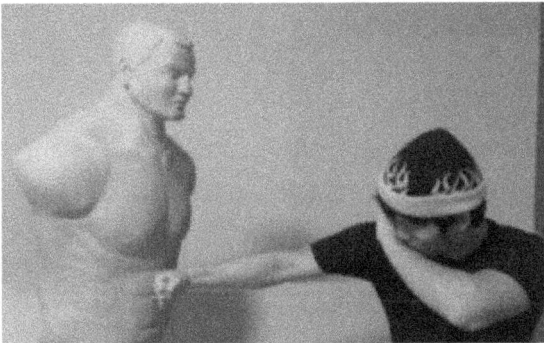

Hammer fist

Those proficient in fighting with weapons, especially bladed or any long weapon that demands the motion of swinging with a tight grip will find themselves adept at the empty-handed translation. Hammer fists can safely strike a hard surface such as an outstretched limb or the skull as it is a naturally padded area of the fist. It can be used as the pommel or the punyo end of the stick when substituting the forearm like a weapon. It may also be flickered out like a back fist jab, though the fingers must be clenched tightly upon impact.

- *Hammer fist into the temple*

- *Hammer fist against the centerline, landing upon the nose or frontal snout.*

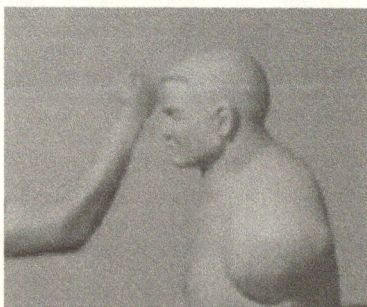

- *Horizontal Hammer fist against the chin, or temple executed tightly to avoid being blocked*

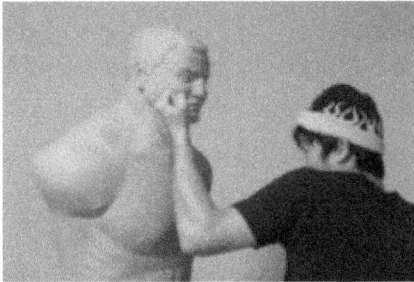

- *Spinning hammer fist combos into the head. Note how forearms and elbows are acceptable alternatives if the hammer fist misses/overreaches. Cover the front of the jaw with the other hand during both swings.*

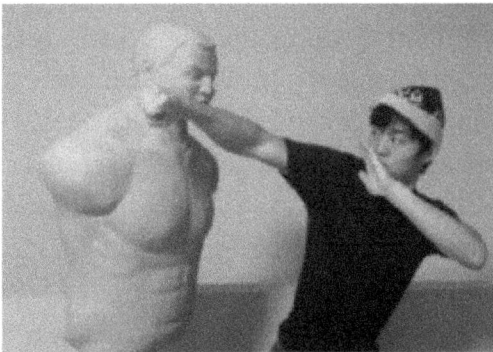

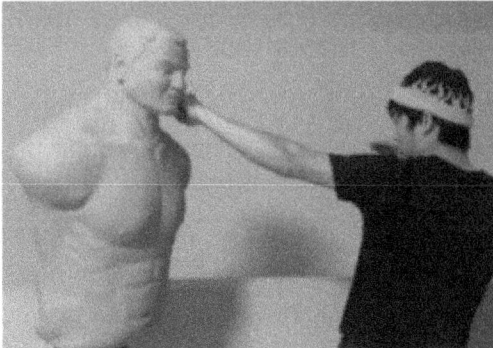

Elbows

Due to the speed of even the most amateur of Ninjas being above those of an Olympic athlete, it is not recommended to use elbows against a Ninja. Unless you somehow have trapped him and have tangled him within your joints on the ground, then it may be fitting to use elbows as finishers for a normal enemy. At best, you will only stun the Ninja, so learn to transition elbow strikes into other moves. Rather than training elbows so often in shadowboxing, forms or katas so that you fight with the mentality of setting combos up to throw them, they should pop out like secret weapons when the enemy least expects it, such as an elbow spiked into the opponent's abdomen as he grabs you from behind.

Aside from blocking, the elbows can bludgeon and spike. Due to the amount of force concentrated on one focal point, the elbow can cut and slice the face open. Do not misjudge distance. Because elbows are executed at such a close range, be sure to always have the other hand up to guard your own face while throwing them.

A holistic method to learn and remember different elbow strikes is to ascribe them into a clock-like system:

- 3 or 9 o' clock would be horizontal elbows, with either lead or rear elbow cutting across the chin or temple (also called a "roundhouse elbow"in some martial arts). Protip: In Thailand, traditional Thai fighters minimize the telegraphing in their horizontal elbows by aligning a shoulder to a wall.

They pop the elbow from the guard directly unto the target, rather than visibly swinging (and therefore telegraphing) the shoulder and pectoral muscles during the movement.

- Elbows that pop directly straight through the enemy's guard *can* be considered 2 or 10 o'clock elbows, but do not travel the entire trajectory across the imaginary clock. These are best visualized as a stabbing thrust into the face.

- Vertical upward elbows are 12 o' clock, slicing the lips and nose or ramming the chin.

- Downward diagonal elbows can be either named for the position they're launched (11 or 1 o' clock) or where they finish their range of motion (5 or 7 o' clock). Do not expose the face too often or too long when launching these, as the tendency to open up the chest and stretch back the shoulders in preparation for a harder strike may become a bad habit during training.

Striking the limb in the interest of disabling it or attacking the nerves, also known as limb destructions, is practiced in nearly all Eastern martial arts and is not recommended in facing the Ninja, who would simply be too fast and would come out the winner in an exchange if you were to elbow his bicep, and he to pluck your eyes out. The thick clothing and adrenaline even for laymen nullifies any pain that is perceived in training and drilling them.

Shoulder

To effectively ram with shoulders requires mastery of internal force, and may require a deep study of Chinese martial arts. Due to the steep learning curve in mastering the body mechanics and using it effectively in sparring, it is a difficult form of striking and not recommended to do. It is possible to transition from a punch, elbow, then into a collapsed into a shoulder in the most extraordinary of circumstances.

- *Ramming with a shoulder from Chinese Xing Yi Chuan is a combination of muscle fluidity and footwork, to say nothing of chi usage.*
- *Pinning with the lead shoulder against the guard or chin of the enemy after a one-two boxing combo, and then tearing in with rear hand body shots or uppercuts.*
- *Pulling the enemy into a shoulder blow from some styles of Chinese Wing Chun.*

Head

Use the crown of the head to bludgeon the face, rather than the apex of the skull or the forehead. A head butt can only be done with careful setting up or thoroughly committed in the observation of a wide opening. That, or when both your limbs are constricted.

- *Pulling the opponent's clothing into the head butt.*

- *A head butt while weapon hand and free hand are locked.*

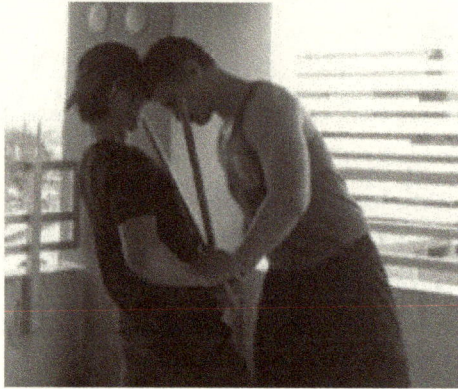

Wrist

Several Chinese Kung Fu styles include wrist strikes (i.e. especially Mantis styles). However, unless one trains specifically in using the wrist as a surface for impact it is discouraged for beginners to be attacking with a wrist, since almost everything we do is tied to our wrists. If the wrists are damaged, everything from holding and manipulating a weapon to forming a structure for a punch is compromised. Long term accumulated damage can take the dreaded form of arthritis or carpal tunnel.

Prevent this by only using the wrist defensively, such as using circular manipulation of movement to receive incoming strikes, and never "folding" the wrist and fist upon impact (align wrist and palm or making the knuckles diagonal).

Legs

Be especially cautious about kicking. Although your legs have more weight to them than your arms, if they are caught or you miss a committed kick, it can mean instant defeat. Become skilled in practical, low line kicks. Flexibility and endurance of the leg muscles must not be neglected. You shall still train in holding out your kicks, strengthening your glutes and abductors as well as your quadriceps, and being able to land a kick at someone slightly taller than you. If you must kick above the opponent's hips, be fast and be certain your enemy is slower than you, or set the kick up with other strikes.

- *The push kick is ubiquitous in all striking arts and is an effective way to create distance or to stop an advancing enemy. Different styles vary in the surface of contact, from the flat of the foot to the toes, to even the heel. To begin learning the motion for thrusting the hips, lie on a flat floor and stick out one leg straight into the air, perpendicular to the ground, the feet of the other leg pressed against the floor. Then push using the other feet and hips only (do not push with hands), stretching the back and training the usage of the hips (this can also be used to train knees). Train to shoot the kick like a Muay Thai push kick, called a "teep," avoiding the telegraphing raise of the knee and shooting forth directly forward into the abdomen or face of the opponent.*

- *The scoop kick can be a transition from a knee, scraping the groin while retracting safely away in one motion. It is essentially a frontal kick aimed at the groin, except instead of fully extending the toe the heel is locked rigid and the foot tucks underneath the knee after making contact with the groin in a swimming motion.*
- *The angle of the oblique kick makes it difficult for opponents to check or guess the target of the kick, which is either the soft inner thigh or the kneecap. Practice the oblique kick's target and hone its accuracy so that you can crush the kneecap completely.*

Knees

A knee, like the elbow, is executed at an extremely close range and should be thrust with either blinding speed or with driving, digging intent with the assistance of the hips. The point of contact must be the spike-end of the knee, rather than the quadriceps. If you do not have the balance to throw a knee from a vacuum, standing on one leg and both hands up in a guard, it is best to simply grab and maintain some form of control on your target and pump knees into his groin or abdomen.

Practice kneeing the groin with explosive speed as taught in most Taichi styles, with the toes raised upwards, expending minimal range of motion but conversely maximum speed. Integrate this speed with your standard Muay Thai knee, now toes pointed downwards, and you will have a more deadly knee to reckon with. You knee the abdomen with hips driving forward, rather than upwards. Or you may pull the opponent's head down into an upward knee.

Grappling

The historical ninja was of relatively short height, thin and most likely did not qualify for anything above a middleweight fight division. If you find yourself gifted in strength and inclined to grapple, tackle, and throw, then perhaps a Ninja would find it difficult to break your bear hug, but that is if you can even make the entry and outsmart his techniques first. If you have somehow managed to get a hold of his head and he is wearing bandanas and cloth or a disguise, ripping it can be incredibly demoralizing to him. Just be prepared for what you see behind the mask, and there is always the risk that revealing the Ninja's identity will cause him to fight with even deadlier fervor and conviction not to let his secret out.

If you find yourself on the ground against the Ninja, something went really wrong. Only proceed with your limb breaks and chokes on this for a single opponent— and even then, you must beware of any weapons on his person. If the terrain around you is hard, gravelly, full of rocks, or concrete, throw him and destroy him. To throw unto the ground is to borrow the earth as a strike.

Arm, wrist or finger locks are realistically only good for exhibitions and impressing strangers at parties. Study foot sectoring and the tangling of legs. If you have caught the opponent's kick, he may be swept. Striking at close range or wrestling in a clinch can transition safely and effectively into the appropriate locks. Many aspects of clinching in Muay Thai may not function effectively outside the ring, with shoes and heavy apparel on. Keep in mind that grappling should be avoided in the advent of multiple and/or skilled enemies.

Foot Sectoring/Crowding

The practice of foot sectoring can be something as simple as Figure A stepping on the toes to stepping on Figure B's outside, preparing for a sweep or restricting movement. All foot sectoring is done with the intention of offsetting his balance.

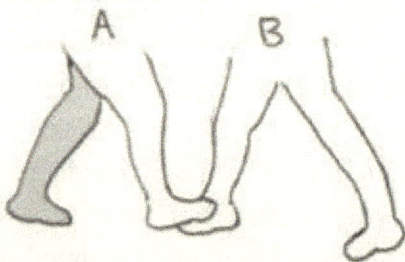

Defense

Footwork

There is a reason why footwork is so highly sought and valued in any sports, and not just martial arts. If a house has a weak base, it will eventually crumble. Mortals are chained to the earth by gravity — the Ninja, however, can become airborne. The most important tool for defense is arguably the most important for offense as well, and it is footwork. How can one strike and avoid being hit in return? Place oneself in the enemy's blind spot. How can one avoid being hit? Not being there.

Principles of footwork vary from style to style (for example, being instructed to navigate on the toes for Muay Thai, the balls of the foot for Western Boxing, and flat-footed for Tai Chi, etc.). Use judgment and experience to determine which is appropriate for the current situation. Overall, footwork should be tactical and efficient. Avoid flashiness; seek subtlety. Constant balance; convey mastery. It is absolutely essential that you train footwork outside within nature, and not just on the sterile-clean, waxed floors of the Dojo. Notice how the terrain affects your footwork, how the environment constricts it and endangers you. Train your awareness and attunement by becoming used to the extraneous rock, the tripping root, the unseen hole or the slippery dirt during drilling or solo-training. How would combative footwork differ in a swamp, as opposed to snow?

Train to be able to close the distance within a target out of range in an instant, while also possessing the litheness to instantly evade. Learn how to step on the outside of an opponent standing with either orthodox or southpaw position (right leg lead). Always aim to step yourself out of the enemy's centerline in order to diminish his accuracy while stepping so that he'll place himself within your centerline. Be explosive in your directional changes. When you observe a fight, whether on media or in person, you shall observe the stances and placement of the participants. Many beginners become preoccupied and enraptured by all the activity occurring in the upper body, and as a consequence overlook footwork. Common errors in their footwork will usually be overextending a limb to compensate not being able to reach; leaning out of balance with the weight unevenly distributed or the head and spine unaligned; they may be standing in too wide of a stance or too narrow a stance; being flat-footed when they are required to be on their toes/balls of the foot, or the incorrect positioning of the feet.

Do not bother imitating so-called, "Ninjutsu footwork." You will be detected and waste valuable time both in training and during the mission. The Ninja at worst scoffs at your attempts to mimic something as secretive and esoteric as his catlike ability to remain silent and still be supernaturally fast while on the move.

Prioritize mastering the knowledge of how to place yourself out of the Ninja's strikes. Learn footwork for weapons-based systems and styles, to avoid the angle and reach of his Ninjato blade or stick. Once you have placed yourself in the perfect angle and within an unbreakable stance for a counter-attack, as an example you can be in a solid, flat-footed stance (i.e. Karate) and deliver a punch drawn from your footing and exertion of chi. If you know yourself to be slow and cumbersome, and cannot find any means to rectify this, you can only hope that reverting to a stiff, solid reliance on earth is a strategy that will leave you surviving.

Blocks/Guarding

Do not spend too much time on blocking during the spur of battle. You may drill blocks endlessly in training, but during the actual fight you cannot allow yourself to slip into a purely defensive mentality. Do not train only on reacting to attack. Doing so will instill the fatal habit of waiting for offense, and never taking the initiative. Wars are never won by defending.

Integrating defensive and offensive head-movement into your arsenal is paramount. Parrying, leg-checking and rotating blocks may never occur within the rhythm of a street fight. Ideally blocking is done as an afterthought or byproduct of having not gotten out of the range of the attack via footwork. Do not bother trapping against the Ninja, whose speed and strength are exponentially superior to yours.

Far more productive use of your time would be to utilize some combative or "offensive" blocking found in several Chinese Kung Fu, Malay and Thai arts and then immediately segue it into an attack, such as the following blocks:

- *Blocking a hook punch with both hands wrapped around the back of the head, both elbows forward almost obstructing your view then stepping forward with the elbow into opponent's face.*
- *Blocking a punch combo with a solid turtle guard from Western boxing, then grabbing the head of the opponent to throw knees in the clinch.*
- *Blocking strikes from all angles in a helmet guard (hands, forearms and elbows encompassing the entire skull to cover 360 degrees), then retaliating with hammer fists.*
- *Missing a punching combo or a large committed punch and immediately covering up in a rhino guard (hands wrapped together resembling slumping one's head on a heap of arms upon a desk, with the elbows frontal and blocking, pushing forcefully into the opponent's space. Be careful of takedowns.*
- *Blocking a low kick with an angled knee, potentially spiking or even breaking the limb.*

You must learn to fall. If, say, you were swept or taken down, landing upon your head is a quick shortcut to bruising the brain and potentially knocking yourself out. Judo is exceptionally useful in learning how to minimize the damage one sustains after suffering a throw from an enemy. Those who truly understand the art can fall on their back upon concrete and feel nigh to nothing from the slam.

Additionally, if you trained under a good master and received proper instruction you can, albeit to a limited extent, negate the damage done to your internal organs from a catastrophic blow by a combination of healing the site of injury with chi and the expelling of torpid chi, done amidst combat in seconds. For more on stances in combat, see "Civilian and Combat Stance."

Multiple Assailants

"Face a single foe as if you are facing ten thousand enemies; face ten thousand enemies as a single foe."
-Morihei Ueshiba, Founder of Aikido

If you have done your preparation prior to an altercation properly, you already are aware where the exit(s) is in a room or the nearest path to safety in a field (See: "Know the Environment"). If you have the common sense and will to live, you will head directly towards it. You must train yourself to think with the mentality of a rodent. What do rabbits, squirrels, cavies, mice and other vermin have in common? The dodging of dangers. The need and talent to escape at all costs. *Why is a cornered animal often the most dangerous to confront?* Ask yourself— who would you rather fight: an individual making the conscious decision to stay and fight, or someone trying to escape? Give an inmate a knife and enter him into a death match and he would not last four men. Present the same felon the opportunity to get past behind the four men to the only exit in the room and he will fight like a beast possessed, far more feral and dangerous than he was armed. You must purge yourself of societal notions of cowardice, honor or face. Banish any concepts of fair fights. Your heart must race with mortal alarm, for the nature of a group attack usually multiplies the chaos factor and aggression beyond the perimeters of rationality. You must not dismiss the possibility that any of these individuals may be concealing a weapon on their person. Of course, with Ninja you are immediately reacting by default under the assumption that he is a walking lightweight arsenal. Even more, you must react with the assumption that the Ninja is definitely hiding multiple companions with him on accompanying the mission should he reveal himself to you.

    If you have no direct line of escape, and you absolutely must fight, know the basic rules of thumb for multiple assailants: align the opponents up to minimize simultaneous attacks from other angles. Do not focus on one particular individual for the entirety of the fight. This is why you must cultivate a separate mentality apart from the paradigm you develop in combat sports, where rules force you to focus your attention upon one opponent. This is when you take greater consideration on the meaning of your katas or forms when training traditional martial arts— switch into a primal mentality of a cornered tiger and renew your form with savage energy. Situations will arise when you may knock out the weakest one as one would remove a pawn from a board of chess, but if you can neutralize a stronger hostile from the get go this is golden. Use the environment to create barriers or to mitigate openings. Be cautious when using a wall in the interest of covering your back, however. Becoming pinned or unable to navigate out of it can mean a fatal mistake. These principles are the same whether for empty-hand fights or with weapons.

Weapon Disarming

Removing an opponent's weapon with just the bare hands is a very overrated concept— having been promoted and emphasized in Kung Fu films and action flicks— and quite dangerous. If you must learn how to divest weapons, learn how to handle knives, handguns, and a baseball bat, which is the most common blunt force weapon and cause of death in the United States. Even then, you must do extensive research on practical and speedy disarms, because it is virtually impossible to take the opponent's weapon from him while it is swinging with lethal intent. Keep in mind the damage to your own arteries and nerves should the edge of a knife graze you in the attempt to disarm from the adversary's grip.

- *Learn two to three basic, quick knife disarms, drill each over a thousand times minimum and keep them fresh in your muscle memory. This does not mean you will fight with the mentality to execute the disarm as your ends to a mean. Be sure to slap the eyes with your free hand during the entry to the disarm.*

- *Rushing in to intercept a bat or other heavy, one-handed weapon before the start of the open-handed swing. Follow up immediately with the appropriate joint locks or strikes.*

Weapons

Join a proper school teaching a relevant style and test theories endlessly in sparring. Nowhere do theories seem to be more rampant and misguided than they do in weapon martial arts. Purchasing trainer versions of your selected weapon is necessary in order to train safely, though be aware that certain nuances and properties may be lost in wielding fake and "safe" imitations (i.e. The student may become complacent or forget to respect the edged side of his rubber, wooden, aluminum or polypropylene knife during drills or solo training). If you truly want to become skilled at a particular weapon, much less master it, you ought to learn the intricacies of each tool from a specialist.

Do not neglect everyday tools and objects. Both you and your foe have improvised weaponry as an option. Learn how to fight and deal with a baseball bat, or a walking cane. In the face of everyday concealed carry, you may want to invest in forearm guards or bullet/stabproof vests, but remember to keep things inconspicuous. Train with weapons that require massive strength so that in facing everyday situations, an ordinary branch or crowbar from the street would weigh significantly less than say, a halberd or a Japanese Kanabo war club. It may be fruitful to study more "feminine" weapons such as the throwing dart, the karambit knife, or the fan in Chinese and Japanese martial arts.

Footwork cannot be understated in its importance in weapon usage. To remain out of reach of the opponent's weapon is better than blocking. A single mistake in a scuffle with weapons is far more punishable than a bout with hands alone. Even modern military and law personnel are taught footwork for shooting! Intent and telegraphing must never occur in your swing. That being said, even the hardiest of souls cannot condition himself to endure a second swing from a club or mallet. Learn the different properties of weapons, from whip-like weapons to bladed ones, all of which have their unique methods of usage and limits. Not only will you study the path and nature of their movements, such as the dangerous ricocheting effect upon a nunchuk's impact, but also the finer details such as a serrated edge versus a straight edge when considering the purchase of a knife (the former of which would make a less clean cut, but good for sawing things such as a seatbelt). Learn the combinations of the particular weapon, and how to attack with it *while moving*. Learn the effective targets, cycling between head, body, hands and legs. Be wary of everything the enemy is hiding- techniques yet to be used, his allies, and concealed weapons. Do not limit your mindset to just your weapon hand- use your free, open hand to grab, strike and manipulate the enemy's weapon, all the while being conscious that he can do it too.

Below are essential skills to master for any practitioner claiming to deal with weapons.

Blocking and Checking the Weapon Hand

After managing to block a strike with your one-handed weapon, seize control of the opponent's wrist or hand with your free hand (also called a "check" or "live" hand in different schools of Filipino martial arts). Proceed with the appropriate follow-up strikes or disarm.

Universal 45 Degree Evasion Angle

Because 90% of the population is right-handed, they will lead with their right leg. Hop diagonally to the left to avoid advancing attack. If you train timing the swing of the weapon with the coordinated movement you can match his swing with a chop from your weapon as well.

Knife Jab

If you must be proficient at one attack with a knife, master the knife jab, which can be done in any grip. Stabbing is scientifically more deadly than a slash, having deeper penetration and the speed to be repeatedly executed. Retract the weapon fast upon executing. Optionally you may raise the rear leg momentarily to obtain the reach.

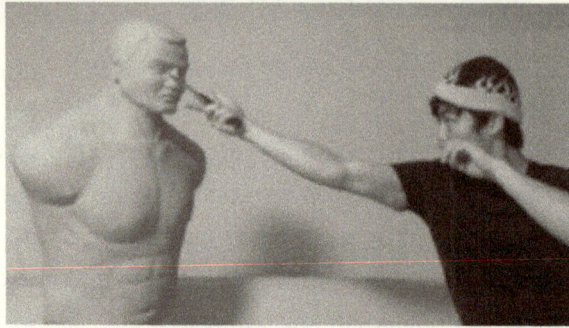
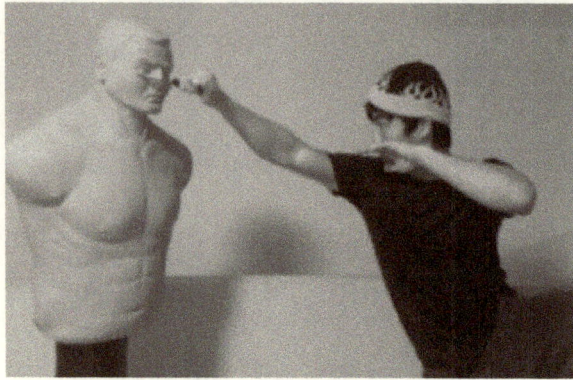

Projectile-Throwing

Throwing a weapon is overwhelmingly committed as the
means to an end. Otherwise, it should be used as a
distraction to get away or to temporarily stun the target to
be engaged in close quarters. Train accuracy and force so
that a knife or axe becomes deeply embedded into its target.
Learn how to throw everyday items from eating utensils,
pencils and pens, a fistful of coins, even your phone or
wallet— from any angle and elevation into the eyes of
target.

      Become fast at throwing heavier objects. It is vital
that you become fluent at tossing everyday objects such as

chairs, in the scenario that you should become attacked in a school or office-like setting. Getting the proper grip for a chair, be it a standard four-legged one or swiveling stool is important, as well as the angle of the toss (over-hand or from the hip). If you are in a rush and need to buy time by throwing obstacles in your pursuer's way, train running and throwing a chair to your side from your hip as if you had switched places with it. If you are throwing it overhand, throw with power, with full intent to crush and knock out the assailant.

Alternatively you can train with bags stuffed with various materials to increase the weight. Training to lift and throw these is a good substitute for anything heavy of an irregular size and shape.

Something to consider: an ordinary playing card can slice through a cucumber; even cut into a watermelon when thrown at the proper angle and velocity.

- *Practice the chambering positions of throwing small objects: Overhand throw of a nail; Throwing pens and pencils from the hip; Tossing debris behind your shoulders, etc.*

Learning how to throw a more deadly weapon such as a dagger or shuriken into a moving target under pressure is difficult, much less than accurately striking areas such as the eyes or throat with it. Practice throwing while on the move, or rolling into the throw.

- *Rolling into the throw with a tomahawk. Becoming familiar with the principles of your weapon means being able to keep it close to your body without self-injury and fear.*

Practice throwing ancient weapons such as the spear, which for millennia was considered the king of weapons before the usage of gunpowder. Of course, you ought to learn the basics of fighting spear to spear, first. Learn how to construct and throw a primitive sling, or shoot a bow and arrow. The last option is to learn how to use firearms.

Self Defense Gadgets

Do not assume that because you are equipped with a tactical pen or key-chain brass knuckle that your fighting skills have automatically been elevated to those of a red belt. Without the requisite skills and proper understanding of weapon usage and experience in using it in drills and/or sparring, the beginner will still find himself swinging with improper body mechanics and clumsy, uncoordinated punches lacking in definitive, aggressor-halting power. Similarly, this truth applies to laymen wielding knives or other, far more lethal weapons.

Though you may buy a tool or self defense product as a novelty gift or as a self-confidence booster, a false sense of security can be fatal. When purchasing, look for a design that is not only durable but one that cannot be used against you, such as a self-defense product disguised as a necklace, which can be improvised as a garrote or choking device by your enemy. As with preparing a bug-out backpack (see "Preparation" under PART 3- The Soul), spare no expenses when it comes to matters concerning your wellbeing.

Common Ninja Weapons

The Ninja is a master of eclectic weapons, and does not make a massive effort to distinguish between "weapon" and "tool." The following is by no means a definitive list, as the purpose here is to demonstrate each design's properties as a unique area to comprehend and master so that, for example, if you can deal with one weapon such as the kunai, then theoretically you can do adequately against a karambit or other combat knife attack. Notice how nearly all the weapons were fashioned from everyday-items or tools, born out of improvisation and necessity during a time when bladed weapons were forbidden in Japan's turbulent feudal history. Poison and chemical weapons are not included, but do not ignore this essential element in the Ninja's gear.

Kunai
This is the Ninja's all-purpose knife for digging and as a close-range tool to stab and slash. Do not engage a Ninja in a knife fight. The Kunai can be thrown.

Kusarigima
A sickle or reaper-shaped blade is attached at the end of a chain. The multitude of functions born from this lethal combination can be used to devastating effect, such as fast and brutally painful chain-whipped attacks, disarms, and hooking motions with the blade. Your weapon may become entangled within the chain of a skilled user, disarmed or simply held in place as the bladed end reaches for your vitals.

Makibishi

Also called "caltrops," these are little spiked traps that could be tossed before a Ninja's mission or during the excitement of his escape. Literal archaeological or historical evidence that caltrops were used by Ninja, but the implications behind the existence of the weapon remain: *do not pursue the Ninja.* If you are somehow following or tracing the steps of the Ninja always look not just up in the trees to your peripherals but also the floor, where the Ninja may have planted traps that puncture and maim the soles of the foot and complicate your task further.

Ninjato

A sword that is much shorter than a Katana, and thus faster and more versatile. When training scenarios involving a Ninjato, the rattan stick used in many South-Asian martial arts is a good substitute for avoiding a Ninjato, as it is shorter than a kendo stick and much faster.

Shuriken

Also called the "Ninja Throwing Star," these little units (which may vary in shape and design) are unable to truly kill unless the thrower has deadly velocity and accuracy, or if the missiles were coated with poison. Use environmental cover or deflection with your own weapon, or agile dodging.

Smoke Bomb/Sand/Powder

Any form of visual obstruction may be thrown as a distraction for the Ninja's escape. They are also used to disorient or to even finish off the opponent. Be careful that

if the Ninja explodes an unknown mist that you do not
inhale, for the chemicals or ingredients used to make the
smoke formula may be noxious and harmful to your lungs
or nervous system.

Staff
Disguised as a simple traveller's walking stick, its range
gives the Ninja a dangerous advantage. The only way to
beat the weapon with the longest range is to have a weapon
with unlimited range: chi projection or a gun. If you
somehow have the footwork, parrying or entry skills to
close the distance, do not assume that you are in the clear,
for the ninja may quick draw his Kunai or tanto knife.
Never assume your foe cannot cut you at zero distance.
Beware of the staff being a concealed shikomizue, which is
a sword sheathed inside a staff-like container.

Tekko-Kagi
Originally used as gardening tools, these claw-like
extensions attached to the hand could vary in length and
design, forming either curved claws or straight hooks for
stabbing, similar to a Katar. Aside from functioning as a
guard, they can rake off the flesh from the victim's face.

Tessen
A blunt-object weapon disguised as a Japanese war fan.
The edge can be steel-edged, though materials used for its
construction can differ. It was traditionally used to signal.
The art of using one to fight came to be known as
tessenjutsu. If a Ninja approaches (presumably in disguise)
with something seemingly benign as a closed fan, be on

your guard. It is lightweight and good for deflection of projectiles.

Civilian and Combat Stance

Nearly every self defense class or seminar teaches a "non-threatening" posture in the face of a possible attack during verbally or physically escalating scenarios, the most common one being the student raising both his hands, palms open as if attempting to diffuse the hostility, around shoulder height. From the space created by the hands (as if he were about to catch a ball toss), he is taught to intercept the incoming punch or he may launch into a strike of his own (i.e. a one-two slap combo). Another common posture resembles Auguste Rodin's sculpture "The Thinker," where the recipient of an increasingly threatening verbal berating places his arms in front of his chest, one hand placed disarmingly on his own face as if sincerely listening, with the other hand cupping the elbow and propping the "thinking" hand up. From this position the student can initiate his own attack or catch an incoming punch to the face (another way to view this is treating the pose as a more benign disguise of the "crab guard" or "Philly shell" implemented in Western boxing).

You cannot walk all day and proceed with your daily activities in a boxing guard or anything so obvious as a wider stance for walking. Ideally you must strike from any position, with either step of your foot taking the lead (train ambidexterity in your stances), or even while one foot is raised mid-step. Erect a simple training target or dummy in your living space so that upon passing by it every day you can strike it quick and hard from a neutral, unsuspecting walking position. Train punching while crouching during your training of shadowboxing, and try to hone the strength of your punches while kneeling or even sitting. Therefore, adopt a separate go-to stance for competitive fighting and an unofficial, pedestrian or "civilian" stance. The most natural would resemble that of standing in wait during a line or for the morning public commute, arms dangled calmly by your sides. Your body is the picture of symmetry, all muscles and ligaments relaxed. Rather than signal to the Ninja that of your obvious background in martial arts training, it will take him by surprise that you can launch a snap of a punch from your hands in your pockets. Use this momentary "turn of the tables" to your advantage and disorient or incapacitate him further with quick, disabling strikes and run (see "Escape").

Fighting Arson

Few people knew that Japanese castles were made of paper. The basic traditional house for cities was but a thin film of highly flammable material. If one house caught on fire, then its neighboring houses were at risk of catching ablaze. Therefore every community back in feudal Japan was technically at risk for a forest fire. Understandably, this is why the crime of arson was dealt with the harshest punishment possible. If an act of arson was able to be traced back to its perpetrator, not only would he be burnt at the stake, his name and very identity would be erased from all records; his family and the cousins of their family and their descendants and ancestors would be slaughtered to compensate for his karmic mistake.

Ninjas are feudal terrorists, in this sense. It only further enforces the awe behind the mask in their willingness to use a weapon with such devastating consequences not just to others but themselves (see "Sacrifice" under PART 4- The Ninja). That being said, a Ninja will be liberal in his usage of pyro-related techniques in any generation, so in preparing to face a Ninja it is imperative that you learn basic safety procedures involving fire. This can be something as basic as understanding principles such as fire needing oxygen to combust, to going the extra step to obtaining fire-proof equipment and apparel. Lose your fear of fire (see "Know Thyself" in PART 1- Mind) without becoming ensnared by the temptations and destructive addictions of the pyromaniac. Pick your battles wisely— perhaps you may find damp, soggy or rainy conditions optimal to confront a Ninja under this mentality. Be ever cautious in your combat applications; locking weapons with a Ninja may mean the risk of him spitting fire directly into your face.

Aerial Attacks

The Ninja will be expected to throw many surprise attacks in the forms of jumping attacks. The closest one can get to practice familiarizing themselves with this would be to regularly spar with a Tae Kwon Do practitioner, although it will be difficult for the kicker to throw spinning jump attacks in a controlled manner and at a full speed in order to fight both realistically *and* safely. What the Ninja can do, however, is far more impressive (and impossible) than 720° spins or kicks that can knock a rider off his horse. He would literally be able to jump over the rider sitting atop his horse. Very few athletes or even the best acrobats in the world are able to replicate such a feat, and due to the scarcity and incredulousness of the act, the target of the Ninja tends to panic and lose track of his assailant during those moments of disorientation. Thus, the Ninja knows how to make tactical usage of his flashy jumps and can even kick during the rotation. This very ability adds an extra dimension and meaning to "footwork," for it is essentially flying. For a vague representation of the idea, numerous vintage or modern *Wuxia* films about swordsmen flying to evade or pursue can portray this lost ability which the Ninja has inherited.

There are several solutions to countering the Ninja's ability to bring the fight to multiple levels. Look up more often. People very rarely look up. They are more or less afraid to look up as you are to look down, from a death-inducing drop. What they cannot perceive from the eyes' range of perception during a walk between the skyline of a city, they are content to proceed the rest of the travel on foot without having ever tilted their neck up to behold the towers, balconies, air and light pollution, or a Ninja about to get the drop on them.

When you start expanding your observation to the Y axis, you are also to a lesser extent training yourself to be ready for ambushes. There still exist traditional martial arts schools today whose masters or senior instructors/students are told to literally ambush a student in order to get the message across to never let down your guard, especially within the confines of their dojo. If you do not have the fortune to locate and be training in such a school, you should get creative with your training. If you have the handwork and craftsmanship, construct dummies whose arms not only represent conventional straight punches, but also imitate punching and kicking from the sky, far above your height. Get used to staring at the unusual sight, and learn the proper footwork to dodge these attacks or counterattack the attack being launched.

ESCAPE

A judgment call must be made on whether it is safe to stop at a chokepoint to rest and glimpse at whom or what is stalking you. If you are able to hide and wait for the threat to pass unaware, do so. If the pursuer has the senses and talent to hound you, flee like a deer. Learning systems like parkour and free-running may be helpful. Focus less on flashy movements and more practical, efficient ones. Learn how to adapt and contort the movement of the body to avoid security measures, or dangling objects such as tree branches. You should not be taking significant time to avoid these obstacles.

Rolling

In the aftermath of a jump or any drop of considerable height, it is necessary to break the fall and possible damage to the ankles and knees with a roll. A gymnastic frontal roll (where the surfaces of contact run straight down the skull and spine) should not be done on concrete. Rather, practice a parkour roll (the contact surfaces running from the shoulder diagonally across the spine). Be able to dive over small obstacles into the roll, such as a table at about waist height. Lose the fear of rolling over harder surfaces such as concrete. Practice the fluidity of this movement so that you may immediately resume running.

Place both hands to preferred position (left or right side, although you ought to be ambidextrous in your rolling as well). Tuck head and the ground should roll over the shoulder. Take note of the distance you cover from rolling.

Vaults

If the object is too big to jump, vault over it and continue once your feet have touched the floor with the same momentum. What is above shoulder height you will have to muscle-up or climb with much haste. Break the training of the vaults into isolated movements/concepts. Practice the movements from a vacuum and then with running with momentum, using chalk or a piece of stick to mark the distance for jumping into the vault. Practice hand placement, and condition your core and flexibility.

- Safety vault

The "Safety" can be done with one hand or supported by both hands, and is given its name for being the most basic vault possible. One foot is on the surface of the object, the other leg tucks between the opening under your body during the transition, ending with shooting the foot propelling both feet forward into the ground.

- Monkey vault

Both hands shoot forward unto the surface of the object, legs tucking through the gap underneath the body. If you are able to do this from a greater distance, it is called a "Kong."

Climbing

Upper Body strength as well as the endurance of the calves is vital for climbing. The less you weigh the less strain on your muscles, particularly your fingers. Be able to hang from your arms for a minimal of five minutes, and be able to do at least 20 pull-ups. You should be able to scale a rope easily. You should climb trees as naturally and half as fluidly as an ape. Imagine out-climbing a bear or cougar for motivation. You should be adept at spotting potential holds and ledges to grip on in artificial, synthetic environments like buildings.

Jumping

Train the explosiveness of the legs with box jumps. Momentum may greatly assist the distance and height of a leap. Practice the precision of jumping onto smaller and thinner landings. Eradicate the natural fear of falling by practicing leaping over reasonable distances atop of injurious heights. When training jumping, you must take care to avoid damage to the knees by not exerting pressure onto them or extending them beyond the toes.

Shadows

People must forget that they ever saw you. Dress unmemorable, act unmemorable, and you shall become invisible. Besides fading from observation, you must deceive, conveying false information to the Ninja gathering intel on you. Thus, one way to remove oneself from a chaotic situation is by guile, secrecy and disguise.

The herd shall obstruct and protect, not just by its numbers but by its pattern. Blending in can mean to act as naturally as possible. Follow the speed of the traffic, rather than exceeding it. Comply with or enable the flow of things, rather than pushing against it. The disappearing man must become steam, liquid, or darkness, in comparison to earth, fire, and light. The following methods can be applied even before detection.

Observe how everyone acts. Don't stick out like a sore thumb. Only follow the herd if need be. Sometimes, you have to make a judgment call, whether in stock-trading or zombie outbreaks. You must have considered all the possible outcomes and consequences before enacting your decision. One choice is to either don their clothing- to act as Romans do. One is to act the complete opposite. When the situation offers a chance, you may deviate from the rhythmic pattern and make your escape (i.e. driving absurdly defensive and conservative, then taking the big risk to rush a yellow light to shake off a tailing vehicle).

Notice all exits in a room or building, ideally before entering. Is that glass breakable in the advent of a fire or ambush? Would that door be easily broken out of, or is it locked for the evening? Can the balcony be leapt from and the landing zone safe and clear? Not all exits are your allies, as they can be used by others as well. Constantly evaluate placing yourself near or far from the exit. Be careful of exposing oneself in front of open exits, as you may put yourself in the Ninja's field of view. In the event of a power failure resulting in total darkness, or should a Ninja should take out the lights, would you be able to make your way to the exit in the dark? In fact, is it even a good idea to take said exit to escape, when it seems to be the most obvious option?

Distractions may be employed from something simple as throwing a penny to something risky and outright dangerous. The toppling of a fragile, loud accident draws multiple people towards the cause of the sound; human nature compels others to gather their focus onto the same spot. Even a sudden verbal exclamation — while giving yourself away — can be a desperate but effective method of getting people to look. Asking or hiring a stranger to assist in a distraction should be one of your last options, for it may cost time, currency, cooperation and persuasion. Even if he does not refuse, your existence and request has given him curiosity about you. You have thus failed to remain invisible in doing so, and have given an individual reason to remember you. There is also the dreaded possibility that he identifies you to the Ninja's future questioning. Fall back on old and true methods, using the elements. A sun glare is reported to be responsible for many traffic incidents still. Distractions can be achieved with the ease of technology or even a classic smoke bomb.

Use cover. This might be the singular most important advice in turning oneself into shadow. Modern warfare military personnel are instructed to remove themselves from the line of fire. At the very least, you must remove yourself from the field of view. Everything natural from foliage to the synthetic is fair game. Make yourself small enough so that your outline does not stick out from behind a desk or pillar. Crouch when passing through windows. Also use everyday items to assist in cover, such as an umbrella or burying your nose in a newspaper. Wear hats or hats that obscure the face. Synchronize your movement and position with the angle and passing of a vehicle. Avoid the trajectory of surveillance cameras.

Of course, you may use literal shadows. Notice the different properties of darkness, how the nature and feel of its dominion differs whether in a rural, urban or wild environment. Use the cover of darkness in the Winter afternoons or twilight hours, but be careful. This is the domain of the Ninja, where he reigns supreme. Be cautious of the threshold between light and dark. Do not break the thin line between darkness and illumination, for you will disturb and contribute your own shadow, which the Ninja will notice.

In the magic of becoming an insentient entity registering no traces of life, you must still your breath. It shall be quieter than a pin drop from a mile away, and be held in the lungs for as long as possible. The pulsations of the heart shall be reduced to a faint murmur, becoming even quieter than the conversation of trees. Think of lunar and nocturnal entities, and strive to borrow their energy or to metamorphose into the owls, bats and the pitch-black expanse of space itself. Because modern technology has the means to spot and read thermals in the darkness, you shall obtain mastery of your internal processes. Lower and cool the temperature of your fingers, forehead and body at will.

If you find yourself suddenly under the spotlight or exposed in public, provide a plausible excuse to exit as to not render the Ninja aware that you became keen of the threat. If you instinctively fall back on the cliché of saying you are lost, you had best provide a good alibi and reason for being in the town/province/area in the first place. If you have not wandered far from your vehicle or public transportation, one example can be to feign ignorance of anything important in the nearby vicinity and that a bathroom break was necessary. If the party which detected you is in allegiance with the Ninja, you need to cause an immediate distraction and escape, or go down fighting.

You must disappear without a trace. A true master will leave behind no footprints, nor a particle of his DNA. The air he displaced with his presence is like a vacuum- no chi or spiritual residue of any kind may be traced backwards to him. There will have been zero evidence of any dimension or material to determine that a person once tread this path. If there were signs of disturbance, they were deliberately planted and caused with intentions to deceive, making it impossible to link their catalyst to you.

Seriously, do not wake up the next morning with a repair bill for the broken window you barrelled out of.

Exercise:
Ever see someone whom you were acquainted with; either just met at a gathering or the previous night, but are not on familiar terms enough— therefore usually culminating in an awkward greeting? If either of you are lost in your thoughts, you could be walking within ten feet on opposite sides of a street before finally making the recognition, during which few precious seconds elapse where one of you may initiate the feeble "Hello!" The next time you sense this about to happen, try detecting the newly-acquainted stranger/colleague first and disappearing completely from his/her awareness before they become aware that you were even shared proximity. The goal is for you to both be on your separate ways, with one of you being none the wiser.

PART 3— Soul

Were this a book for scholars, it would encourage the path
to sagacity through wisdom and virtue. Were this a book
for warriors, it would put much more emphasis on scientific,
detailed information about the human body and how to
manipulate it. Yet, what separates the Ninja's mindset from
the rest is the color of his soul, which is blackened from
vigilance, suspicion, distrust, cynicism and skepticism, all
of which kept him alive to this point, and for eternity. The
Ninja is the best of both worlds. He does not limit and
throw all his stones into the acquisition of knowledge or the
training of the body. He may not be the master of the pen,
nor the sword, but he will outwit the barbarian and kill the
intellectual.

In the interest of being able to match a Ninja, you
would waste little time in attaining values such as honor, or
benevolence. If we must begin the arbitrary practice of
categorizing principles, we can group the offensive spy arts
into deception, distraction and destruction. The more
defensive, or stagnant activities which one enjoys in his
spare time, all while keeping the ultimate enemy in mind,
amounts to the bastion of preparation.

You must never succumb to the obliteration of pain,
psychological warfare or defeat. Prepare now by making
your own personal oath forbidding your loss and death at
the Ninja's hands. The Ninja has already taken his:

> *"Under extreme physical incapacitation or threat of death; even should I fail my mission: I swear that I shall not and will not die. By the honor of my Lord; by the memory of my ancestors; by all that is sacred or profane I forbid my body or spirit to perish."*

Daily Conduct

This chapter concerns the immediate personal conduct and vigilance in everyday life. Check corners before entering an elevator. Learn a good close-quarters striking art for enclosed, claustrophobic spaces. Do not drive like an idiot. Create as little stimuli around you as possible— you shall become a stimuli EMP. Eyes and attention should pass around your silhouette like North and South ends of magnets repelling each other. Like the legend of vampires not appearing in reflections, you shall extricate yourself from the memory film of others.

"The essence of the day lies in the morning, that of the year in spring, and that of one's life in diligence."
-Zhu Xi, Neo-Confucian Scholar of the Song

Consistency is the hallmark of discipline. In Japanese, the word "kaizen" in business refers to continual self-improvement, the concept having now been applied to psychology, life-coaching, and banking. It is about purposely, regularly solving the obstacles in one's life, one-by-one. Rather than solving things overnight, a single change would be overtaken and maintained until it has become habit. You cannot be hyper-vigilant for one week then relax your lifestyle for the next. Relaxation is temptation. This is the precise moment a Ninja waits for in observing his subject to carry out his plans. Do not allow yourself to degrade to filth and homeliness. You shall not give away your presence by unpleasant odors or artificial ones. Ideally you become scentless. This is why grooming and cleanliness is essential. Maintaining a consistent routine for sleep will be critical in ensuring that your tasks for the day are accomplished on time and with energy. The General Zeng Guofan who lead the Imperial Armies in suppressing the Taiping Rebellion wrote, "For the past two centuries, our virtuous predecessors have made it a habit to get up early. Even in cold winter, my great-grandfather was said to rise an hour before the sun, and my father at sunrise." He woke up every morning at 4 am.

In contrast, appearance may be the only thing that may be inconsistent. Become a master of disguises. Wear sunglasses only during daytime or when feigning blindness. Switch between different fashion betraying varying socioeconomic and personal aesthetics. Hats are excellent. Alternate hairstyles or wigs. Be aware of clothes that make too much rustling noise. Remember to dress with the intent to deceive.

"He who is learned does not look erudite; he who looks erudite is not learned."
- Chapter LXXXI, *Dao De Jing*

Body language can be interpreted individually or macrocosmically. Read the situation and plan ahead accordingly. The epicenter of an incident from several blocks away can ripple through people's actions like a stone dropped into a body of water. Look up the OODA loop which they teach to American Air force pilots. Do not give eye contact- locking eyes, even a momentary second, can be a great way to trigger the stimuli in people's brains and allow people to remember you. Depending on the environment and situation, adopt either a meek, submissive posture, a neutral, grounded one or a tall, confident walk of openness.

Control your mouth. Not a single philosophy in this world advocates talking more and listening less. Being multilingual really helps, in comprehension and making things difficult for the locale to understand you. While the optic canals may be the most greedy of senses, your tongue is the most generous organ of communication, in that it simply gives and gives without tiring. You will leak much of your opinions, insecurities and other information you do not want others to know through the slip of a tongue, an unwanted and unsolicited remark, and so on. Some Ninjas are completely silent, from the moment of their oath to their death. While talking may help you navigate out of a dire situation, at most it can only inhibit you.

Incorporate your martial arts training into your movement and philosophy in daily life. How does the Taichi tripodal stance help you with balance on the public commute? How does the peek-a-boo slipping from boxing help you duck low-hanging tree branches and other head-level obstacles? How does Filipino eskrima footwork enable you to avoid bumping into people? How does the pacifist philosophy of Aikido enable you to diffuse the situation and render strangers into friends instead of enemies? Are you able to walk behind someone quietly so that they are unaware you are behind them?

Train your eye and spirit to detect aberrations in the normalcy of things.

Exercise:
Train your ability to spot differences. Scan the array and spot the wrong letters immediately. Is it easier with another language?

FFFFFFFFFFFFFFFFFFFFFFFFFFFFFFFFFFFFFFFFFFFFFFFFFFFF
FFFFFFFFFFFFFFFFFFFFFFFFFFFFFFFFFFFFFFFFEFFFFFFFFFFFF
FFFFFFFFFFFFFFFFFFFFFFFFFFFFFFFFFFFFFFFFFFFFFFFFFFFF
FFFFFFFFFFFFFFFFFFFFFFFFFFFFFFFFFFFFFFFFFFFFFFFFFFFF
FFFFFFFFFFFFFFFFFFFFFFFFFFFFFFFFFFFFFFFFFFFFFFFFFFFF

戌戌戌戌戌戌戌戌戌戌戌戌戌戌戌戌戌戌戌戌戌戌戌戌戌戌
戌戌戌戌戌戌戌戌戌戌戌戌戌戌戌戌戌戌戌戌戌戌戌戌戌戌
戌戌戌戌戌戌戌戌戌戌戌戌戌戌戌戌戌戌戌戌戌戌戌戌戌戌
戌戌戌戌戌戌戌戌戌戌戌戌戌戌戌戌戌戌戌戌戌戌戌戌戌戌
戌戌戌戌戌戌戌戌戌戌戌戌戌戌戌戌戌戌戌戌戌戌戌戌戌戌

You should be able to detect immediate deviation from patterns and routines. Individuals, diseases and abnormalities should stick out to your eye like a blip on modern radars. Be suspicious of what you eat. Check to see if anything smells bad or has been tampered with. For this reason, you should keep enemies close. It is easy to grow complacent and secure about the loyalty and unobserved lives of your allies. You must be able to detect changes in friends' conduct or speech- have they sold you out? Are you able to deduce their causes from their behaviors alone?

Become skilled at ancient methods of prognostication or forecast. Be familiar with old wives' tales or traditional ways to interpret the firmament and Earth. Trust in Heaven and your fellow beasts, while also respecting their autonomy. The smallest of beasts can betray your location, for example. Observe how animals react before a coming storm. Why did your pet reject the food you placed before its nose, despite on appearance and technicality it is edible for you both?

Meditation, like many of the skills in this book, is a subject that will need its own volume. From meditation and the internal arts of chi gong, you learn to relax and strengthen the organs of the body you cannot target in a gym. Keep a clear mind. The personal values and cults individual Ninja subscribe to vary, but the overlapping theme for their beliefs is ultimately *death*. Thus, you shall believe in life. Though you will not neglect lunar energies and influence, you shall not forget your diurnal roots and maintain your relationship with the sun. Visualize success, but also be wary of consequences of failure, which is one of the few human concepts that a Ninja may actually fear. Internal self improvement through autosuggestion and self-hypnosis were all techniques used by the historical Ninja.

Deprivation. Fast to strengthen body and mental fortitude. How long can you survive without food in a disaster? Can you out-starve your enemy in war? Frugality is a treasure. But it is not just the material corpus that needs to train itself through deprivation. Deprive yourself of wanton indulgences. Rid temptation and instant gratification from your way of life, whether it be cutting excessive sugar from your diet or mindless gaming. If you have an insatiable itch to befriend strangers, to talk to friends, to make the business of others yours, then you need to become used to being lonely. Do not fidget or have your heart race while meditating or studying in a quiet room occupied solely by yourself.

Constantly adapt. Your techniques will evolve and you will ever be building new skills depending on the age you live in. Do you know how to hotwire a car? How about working the elevator system? This leads to the next section....

Technology

There is barely a soul untouched by the influence of a computer today. The education of millions and their careers are indelibly linked to a computer so that making one's bread is impossible without possessing and using the internet. Even millions who primarily use the World Wide Web to search, abstaining from posting on social media or even owning email accounts, may still unwittingly be "giving" their secrets to malware and third parties interested in their personal info. Even without having ever sent a message online, much can be learned about a person from their browser history alone. In this sense, a computer is a digital appendage as loathsome as the tongue. More often than it is helpful, both easily betray and give ourselves away. Even worse, it is arguably more addictive than the act of talking alone. You should not form a parasitic, symbiotic relationship with your desktop or laptop, for the sedentary life is inimical even to the way of the scholar.

A competent or frightened warlord would not settle on just a wall around his settlement. Nor would he be satisfied with the amount of traps and the moat surrounding his castle. He sleeps every night with the anxiety of knowing he can improve the security of his kingdom with something, anything, just to make the work of Ninjas a little more difficult. Thus you must do everything possible to make it harder to penetrate and uncover your passwords and accounts. Vigilance must be consistent, and complacency and laziness are the enemy. Learn how to use key-authenticators, in the unlikely event that your device for confirming entrance is compromised. Get the top notch encryption for your digital address: create a protonmail.com email address. Not even the creators can read your messages, and if you do not provide a back-up email to your account it will be lost forever, which is a good thing.

An enemy operative would, in the process of "knowing the enemy" be recording every word one is typing in a confidential email *as it is occurring*. Even if the content or moment is something as innocuous as conversing freely with a friend online, becoming familiar with the subject's online persona and how one speaks online is information that the Ninja will exploit. Those who spy on the business generated from your keyboard are known as "key loggers." Downloading a Key Scrambler is a simple and quick solution to this problem, which jumbles your encrypted keys to those potentially trying to gather intel on you.

Apply for alternate forms of currency. There are millions praising the convenience of China's heavy reliance of using electronic apps to pay for everything. These people are reprehensibly stupid. Should a citizen anger the mainland government, they will find that the meaningless numbers on their phone were nothing, having been canceled or drained by the powers that be. Soon they will desperately long for the comfort of crumpled bills in order to pay for a single fruit in a market stand. Next they might regret failing to cultivate survival skills or heeding the old adage: "The nail that sticks out is the one that gets hammered down." Whether or not one buys into the democratic philosophy behind Cryptocurrency, a decentralized mathematical system such as the blockchain makes it virtually impossible for hackers or current governments to tamper with the system. Besides investing into Bitcoin, one might also want to secure his finances abroad such as opening a Swedish bank account.

In history and play, warriors, messengers and spies have burnt and eaten the letters or codes they hid on their person in order to avoid the information falling into the wrong hands. The application for the digital world is to implement a fast method to delete everything in case everything goes south. Having a one-key button and a secret password for confirmation may be all it takes to wipe a hard drive of its contents.

Preparation

The essence of madness is different for the two sexes. For men, it takes form in the manifestation of paranoia, and it is not necessarily a bad thing. Preparation against unlikely, yet-to-be dangers and even imaginary enemies is preferable in most cases to being apathetic or ignorant of how to deal with the threat once it manifests and becomes your problem. There is no definite list to preparing for the arrival and fight with a shadow warrior, but the following essay lists suggestions which to form a solid basis for your defense.

A Bug-out Bag is one of the quickest, convenient solutions one will get to having comfort, security and survivability in one, compact location. To an extent, it is masculine paranoia personified in materialism. In the advent of a natural disaster, or in case a Ninja burns down your village or home, whether buried under rubble from an earthquake or fleeing into the wilderness the most immediate thing you need to bring with you is your bug-out bag, which has all the tools and equipment necessary for 72 hours of survival.

Not all bags are the same quality. It can be anything from a vintage British Special Ops kit or a strapped one used by the army. When choosing a bag, do not settle on cheap, inexpensive material whose straps would break under lots of weight and exertion. Never settle for less in the interest of your self-preservation. Water should be the first thing you put in your bug-out bag. Then non-perishable or well-preserved rations should be next. Content should be selected based on an individual's climate, with the appropriate tools or clothing prepared to help one survive in a boggy swampland or dry, arid desert. Do not spend too much time on picking knives or weapons for your bag, as a tough, sharpened blade that does not rust is all you need. Your bag should not be so burdened that you find it difficult to climb or run. There exist many resources in books and the internet on building the suitable bug-out bag for your specific location and needs.

Strive for self-sufficiency in all avenues of your life. This can mean anything from home-grown food to raising livestock like chickens for eggs and meat. Maintain your link with your ancestors' rural or pastoral ways, for your peers have long forgotten them. The Ninja has not. He is counting exactly on your ignorance and modern complacency; he would cut off trade routes or bomb the local market to wage a siege against your stomach. Improvisation is an underrated yet highly valued trait. If tools or funds are scarce, nature can provide the solution. Learn skills such as constructing and forging tools or weapons from nature.

Castles and fortresses were full of traps to deter enemy soldiers and Ninjas. They need not be lethal or deleteriously crippling so much as they needed to make the defenders aware of where the intrusion is happening. Disguise made them all the more effective. A specific manner of laying tatami mats called *mawashijiki* enabled a soft "swish" noise to occur when Ninjas would hug the wall in an attempt to avoid any traps laid in the center of a room. Pay particular attention to thresholds, such as doorways, as well as open-spaces such as gardens or halls. Once the Ninja has braved all these challenges, you will be forced to rely on immediate, personal action. You need to find suitable and convenient locations for hiding your weapons, both antiquated and modern in your domain. Find the balance between accessibility and secrecy. Do not reveal or display weapons in the open.

> *Uguisubari,* translated as "nightingale floor" alerted the Shogun with a loud creak where an enemy spy's footsteps disturbed in the middle of the night. His men were trained to hear specifically for this sign of intrusion.

Perhaps the best kind of trap or security measure may be owning and raising a dog. Some scrolls advising stealth and thievery have specifically warned to avoid triggering the bark of a guard canine for their augmented sensitivity, with hearing and smell magnified many times that of humans, as well as even a primal sort of sixth sense. For this reason Dogs have been historically considered the enemies of ninjas for many clans. Beware that, like the modern man, domestic dogs can have their savagery and any combative instincts bred out of them. Even pitbulls have been observed to fail to defend their owners and stimulated burglary/intruder scenarios.

You must take anti-darkness measures. It goes without saying that one immediately becomes wary, especially at night. Do you have alternative light sources when the power goes out? This should be one of the most important lessons in this book. A Ninja makes the darkness his home. The ancient Chinese wisdom of *feng shui* (also known as Chinese geomancy) always stresses that the spots of the room, like missed patches of dust, which receive minimal or no light should be exposed and brightened. Thus, you shall lighten the darkest corners of your room with lamps, reflecting mirrors, LED lights, candles, UV-A lights, or any means possible. Provide emergency lighting should these sources be snuffed out, or the power is disabled.

There can never be a complete list on preparing a fortification or home for a Ninja attack. Remember that your lack of imagination will kill you.

PART 4— The Ninja

Stand strong before the ultimate enemy, more merciless and efficient than any tyrant. If you presented your jugular on a platter, be assured that he would take it. Warnings and a fair fight conceptually do not exist for him. Although he does not put a premium on sadism, if needed he would torture you for the information his job demands.

You must cultivate the mindset needed for facing this opponent at all costs. Do you know how to react to a basic Angle 1 sword slash in the Filipino Martial Arts? Do you know how to counter a roundhouse kick? The ultimate opponent has endured more hardships than you have, and each one was more deadly and unfathomable to your sheltered, 21st century mentality. He has meditated under freezing waterfalls, gazed before perilous cliffs, while also burying himself alive for nights and walking on burning coal barefoot. He has starved himself on leaves and insects, ravaged his body with poisons and drugs. He has broken every bone in his body, and sacrificed a few digits or his facial features in order to succeed in his missions. He knows every deed and name of his ancestors, and is completely willing to forget a brother who shames the family lineage.

Can you muster an ounce of the strength to go through what he has, to experience the bitter elements he endured, in order to achieve even a remote, tip-of-the-iceberg understanding of his blackened mind and soul?

Ideally, you prepared yourself so that you can avoid a physical confrontation with a Ninja. If you find yourself about to engage in mortal combat with one, something went deadly wrong with your preparations.

Once defeated, your weapons disabled and your joints broken, his blade resting on your throat, do you think sorrowful pleas or guileful rhetoric can dissuade the Ninja from finishing the job? Do you think you can bribe a Ninja to betray his contract and masters into not finishing his task? Do you two even speak the same language? Perhaps he really is a demon in the guise of a four-limbed human, at which this point not even knowing Japanese may save you.

Perhaps your only comfort lies in the fact that the perfect enemy does not exist. In some religions, such as the Abrahamic religions this archenemy is the Devil. What if one day you were to face the next worst thing? He may not be supernatural or twisted beyond all logic, but he is still skilled enough to get the job done, and that job is to neutralize you. Only the arrogant flatter themselves in thinking they can escape a Ninja. The scholar thinks himself able to outwit one, while a warrior fancies himself strong enough to best him. You had best be prepared and ready to face the threat.

Darkness is His Home

If there is a single lesson, a most immediate takeaway you can apply to your training philosophy from this book it should be the concept of darkness. Release all of society's preconceived notions and associations of the dark with the immoral. Immerse yourself both physically and figuratively in your study of darkness. Embrace the Daoist concept of the "yin" half, and learn to respect the dark.

Respecting the dark begins with understanding its power over you, and your own limitations. You will be reminded of your slavery to the most dominant of the five senses every time the darkness holds dominion. You will never completely eradicate the fear of the unknown deeply embedded in your reptile cortex of your brain. You cannot see completely in the dark, for you do not have an owl's eyes, and even owls cannot see without the tiny assistance of light. You can never match the Ninja's mastery of the dark because he is not mortal.

And that is why you must train to overcome this disadvantage. Protect and preserve your vision that the rods and cones in your retina may be able to discern the finest lines in the dark, given what mercifully little light you have. Consume foods and nutrients that are good for the eyes. What the most important sense fails to provide, the other senses must be strengthened in order to survive. The ears must become attuned to the slightest pin drop; a creak in a corner of the house; the flap of a moth's wings. The nose must be able to discern the change in the quality of the room air as a result of the new visitor (or intruder). Train your sensitivity in wearing a blind-fold, and navigating around the refines of your room, if you do not already train a martial art which implements blindfold drills (for example, Wing Chun). Get used to stubbing your toes, and bruising your knees. Hone your chi to be able to sense the life force or spirit of animate and inanimate things.

Become familiar with the dark, but do not seek out the dark often. Why would one fight a shark in its own territory: water? Respecting the dark means you understand how the dark can serve you, while always being mindful of how it can elude and ruin you. Shadows are created by light. Be aware that the flashlight and weak, dim lights flickered on in response to the onrush of complete blackness due to the workings of a Ninja will potentially create more cover and assistance for your foe.

Between You and a Ninja

"Shall I make spirits fetch me what I please, resolve me of all ambiguities perform what desperate enterprise I will? I'll have them fly to India for gold, ransack the ocean for orient pearl, and search all corners of the new-found world…"-Faustus, *The Tragical History of the Live and Death of Doctor Faustus*

The Ninja have been glorified and thus fed stronger by their peers and modern pop culture. They were rightfully seen as demons. His art has trained him to blend and control the filthiest dregs of society. He is comfortable amidst the execrable and accursed, and thus makes his camp among the foulest and lowest residents of slums.

A Ninja's mentality is rather simple in his approach to his mission: Get from point A to point B. Obtain X and Y. Use whatever means possible to get the task done. He will maintain all other priorities such as remaining unseen and unnoticed if need be, but his primary goal must be achieved at all costs. He will not go out of his way to finish the job in a more creative or morally acceptable method if it means it will be done in an instant. Because the Ninja has a supreme understanding of and operates within the Dao, nothing material nor magical may impede him.

Fatigue does not exist in a Ninja's mind. His muscles will give out long before his will does. There are no barriers you can erect to place between yourself and a Ninja. You can run indefinitely, but you definitely cannot hide. The most cutting edge of modern traps and weapons are rendered toys under his grasp and efforts. The toughest security will be dispatched as if a rock through a spider's web. Rest assured that if a Ninja were tasked to locate a singularly guarded penny locked in Fort Knox, he will eventually secure it. The most elusive and dangerous man who thinks he can evade the system forever eventually becomes discovered by the Ninja. His dogged persistence means that his undertaking of the mission will never cease until it is either finished, or he is.

Sacrifice

Your theoretically perfect foe has a bloody, shameful history that would curl the stomach of anyone unfortunate enough to hear it. He has sacrificed everything to reach perfection, his dark *Dao*. He had forsaken the material world in devoting his waking hours to the perfection of his art. He had renounced his religions and faith in witnessing the countless perversions occurring in his missions and behind the scenes. He has lost hours of sleep, thus shaving years off his longevity, and has done incalculable damage to his body. He has experience with prisons and survived each of his sentences. He has stooped to drinking the blood of animals to settling for his own urine and feces during times of desperation. He has suffered and survived many stab wounds to his feet, legs, and torso and has emerged stronger from each one. He has cut his tongue and crushed his vocal cords so that he may never speak again. He has scarred and maimed his own face so that he may wear any disguise on top of his dented skull like a glove. He didn't think twice about severing a digit as a price for failure or being caught, and many would leave it at the loss of a limb as the penultimate sacrifice in service to a mission or lord.

The Ninja has done far more than sacrifice his own individual in his path of the dark *Dao*. In fact, there is not a single culture which does not deem sacrificing oneself as ignoble or deplorable. The concept of taboo does not exist for a Ninja, however. In his unshakeable will and resolve, he has committed what countless religions and teachings consider an indelible sin: He has sacrificed the well-beings of others.

He has betrayed his masters and several clans in defecting to a more advantageous one. He has exploited and lead to the ruination of his friends and lover's family in the interest of self-gain. He had killed his own parents when orders or circumstances required it. He had left his brothers to die under threat of being compromised in a mission. He has strangled his own infant in mid-scream to remain undetected. He has burnt every last branch of his family tree for the price of failure. Having no filial roots, he is truly, completely alone in this world which, unsurprisingly, has proved quite a boon to him: He cannot be threatened, and he has nothing to lose, at least, by our conventional, mortal standards.

Cold-Blooded

Does the sight of blood make you light-headed? Do you frown in disapproval and relief that a distant war is occurring in another continent, far away from home? Do you grimace or protest in indignant rage when you see a fight ensue in public? Can you stomach beating your dog, much less your child? However we like to convince ourselves that these physiological reactions are symptoms of our morality, the Ninja has only one word for it: weakness, and weakness is an emotion that has long been wringed out of his system during his training. By day he may be Buddhist, but he is aware that during a contract, morality and fatality are mutually exclusive and not of the same coin. In some cases, what may evoke hesitation or revulsions for the average, law-abiding citizen has warped into perverted delight for him. He does not care for the amount of tax dollars required in undoing the damage he causes in his wake. He would torch your domain or headquarters in an instant if necessary. He does not quantify the long-term consequences on the environment as a result of his actions into his decision-making. He does not care about the hundreds of commuters he will make late in disabling the public transportation system. He does not care to spare the mental trauma he will inflict upon bystanders and onlookers to his soon-to-be-carried-out-deeds. He would not hesitate to spill and paint the walls of your house with your blood. He would not think twice of using your children for hostage or, Heaven forbid, spilling theirs in convincing or destroying you.

Nietzsche's famous quote "In fighting a monster, we must ensure we do not become a monster ourselves" may seem necessary to bring up here. Nevertheless, sometimes, we must journey into the heart of darkness so that we may endure real darkness, not wholly unlike the concepts or mechanism of flood therapy or a vaccine. You do not need to throw away your humanity, but you need to toughen your stomach against the evils of the world.

Accomplishing this can begin with the smallest of actions. Watch horror movies. Eat raw meat. Don't refuse an offered fight. Read on the deeds of serial killers. Participate in combat sports. Visit a slaughterhouse, or an actual battlefield.

Human

The Ninja assumes an exterior of extreme stoicism and/or apathy in the face of every evil of the world. To rouse the passions of a Ninja is like striving to awaken the spirit of a mountain eons old, with a critical difference: the Ninja is, in several senses of the word, dead. He took all the possible qualities which make him vulnerable and human and forced them into the contents of a box, which he buried in a secret location of a forest. Through strong mental drills and the sovereignty of time, he made himself forget the location. Even should the forest be razed to ashes, the box will remain buried under it. He conceals anguish and delight within the labyrinth of his psyche. His gaze is straight and piercing in the face of threats and opprobrium. His armor of guiltlessness is a hide that repels the arrows of conscience, as well as any notion of salvation. Though he is able to sense the attraction or enmity of others, he only feels it in relation to his mission, as a means of gathering and interpreting stimuli. He is not encouraged nor weakened by feeling these emotions of his peers, nor does he ruminate upon them once the sensibility has passed.

No one understands the Ninja, and this does not bother him. Unlike you, he does not share the fundamental human need for sympathy or pity. Because a Ninja has forsaken his humanity, you must conversely do everything possible to latch unto yours. A Ninja's list of follies during childhood is short, because they have been spotted and eradicated on the spot. You must cherish the memories and naiveté of your childhood- let it be a damper of courage against your final moments against the Ninja. Never lose your treasures of compassion, mercy, and forgiveness.

In facing a Ninja in combat, overwhelmingly the odds are that you must paradoxically give up all your human qualities. Let fairness and mercy be extinguished from your consciousness at the moment. The Ninja's traits and approaches the warrior finds cowardly and pathetic. But the Ninja knows these extra lengths ensure his victory. That is why you must learn his methods and have the judgment to use them against him, whenever possible. But the moment you have somehow wrenched his goal from his hands moments from his completion of the mission; when you make your escape; when you somehow impossibly find the thread of his life within your hands, let him know that it was because you were human- that you possessed something that he did not- that enabled you to win.

Part 5- Psychology

Strengthen your mental fortitude. Be aware that the Ninja is aware of all of these methods so take care not to have them used against you. All of the concepts are obviously linked to one another.

Legend Aura

Capitalize on your own fame, appearance and hype. It is of enormous advantage to possess the reputation of a good fighter. Are you of Asian descent and your opponent has (not entirely unfounded) notions of you as an Oriental legend? Do not let his assumptions, or rather, do not let your illusion be shattered. Assume that extravagant kung fu pose before engaging to gain the momentary psychological upperhand. Snarl and glare like the barbarian brawler you seem to be. Traditionally Muay Thai fighters are trained, even in modern gyms today, to act as if a blow inflicted upon them never happened. This means when you take a jab to the face, you snap your head back into position as if there was no damage received at all.

      The stuff which composes "Legend Aura" are not limited to: memories of past conquests, rumors or gossip of one's physical prowess, official fight records, ethnic and cultural stereotypes in regards to behavior and appearances, and confidence. It is the awareness and complete acceptance of one's role in the complex web of human relationships, both real and perceived. It is the exploitation of the environment, and comes from ample understanding of the culture and history of the vicinity (see "Know the Environment").

To claim that you are master of a deadly art and maintaining a lethal stance makes amateurs mentally crumble during a sparring session. Mentioning at the crucial moment that you train in a respected martial art can stagger the expectations of certain individuals. View the strength of your own aura as a mental form of armor, one which mysteriously parries punches that would have landed from your face, or stifling the opponent's aggression with invisible pressure. In some cases, they completely lose the will to fight. It is unsurprising that a fighter will fare worse against a peer whom he knows to be a national champion rather than if they were sparring in a friendly match as complete strangers.

Superstition

"Learn to trust reason and your senses, and you will then be
worthy of my attention."
- Marquis de Manzinni, *A Sicilian Romance*

Many dismiss the premise that superstition is a condition of human existence, and foolishly assume they are immune to its charms. There are studies that show that even atheists believe in magic to an extent. Therefore you shall exploit the enemy's superstitions. What religion is he? If you were unable to collect intel beforehand, take an educated guess on what he or his people believe in. Spread rumors beforehand which will somehow indirectly make it to him, clouding and affecting his judgment. It is an enormous advantage if you have no religion of your own, which is why you must guard yourself against attacks against superstition you did not know you possessed.

Does he believe in demons? Of what kind? Denounce and blaspheme the trinity with no qualms for you possess the advantage of not believing in their Gods. Sometimes an enemy warrior gives away his beliefs by the designs on his skin, clothing or armor. Some individuals form a strong attachment or belief to religious talismans, such as the scapular for Catholics, or a knife for those of the Sikh faith, of which divestment and stripping the wearer of these items can be profoundly demoralizing. If you acknowledge that you yourself are nevertheless vulnerable to these sorts of mental attacks, it may be of more use to "play within the same rules": learn voodoo counter-spells. Make daily prayers, mantras, or spells of protection from malevolent ones. The trick is to be *selective* in your superstition. Become an atheist when black cats cross your path or when you become witness to other inauspicious signs. Become agnostic and delighted when fortune appears to smile upon you. Believe during these moments that you are the master of your own fate. Therefore it is prudent to not assume a lifestyle of gambling or anything which encourages superstition in your own character, for it is difficult to separate luck from fate.

Emotional Assault

One beautiful definition of Hell comes from a Buddhist parable: A samurai asks a wise monk to show him the ways of Heaven, but upon being refused, the samurai threatens the monk with death under the influence of hot anger. The monk calls this hijacking of emotions: "Hell," whereupon the samurai recognizes the wisdom of the monk and bows for forgiveness (to which the monk observed: "and that, is Heaven").

You shall bring your enemy to Hell. Then attack him from Heaven, while he is entrapped in Hell, clouded by his escalated emotions. Provoke the enemy and insult something he really cherishes. If you did your research in knowing the enemy beforehand, you would know what his mental Achilles heel is. This can be anything from his Gods, offspring, a lover, to his ego. A few choice selection of creative insults or swear words may be all it takes to destabilize a weak mind.

Belief in Oneself

The word "placebo" originated from the Latin phrase "I shall please." Those who claimed a false relationship with the dead in order to get free food were thus called "singers of placebo" around the 17th century. Placebo medicine may be simple sugar-water pills disguised as medicine composed of the proper curing ingredients and chemistry, and yet produce the same positive effects as a real one. Quack medicine, acupuncture, and many "home cures" or traditional medicines are all considered to be demonstrations of the placebo effect. Astoundingly, repeatable studies reveal that even though people knew or were informed that something they were about to receive were a placebo, the false medicine still worked, simply from the power of belief. Similarly, a "nocebo" engendered detrimental health effects simply from the expectation that something would cause injury or sickness, such as the false assumption of having ingesting poison.

The powers of hypnotism and autosuggestion are thus open to your disposal as you see fit. The body assisted and elevated by the mind is evident in the mind-body connection from activities such as yoga to weightlifting. Some historical Ninja wrote characters evoking the attribute (such as "water") that they wanted to adopt upon the palms of their hands, then swallowed the imaginary word while chanting the word verbally and in the mind.

If you believe in your own legend, the strength of your motivations, the justness of your own cause, you will avail. Believe yourself to have a body of iron, as if the excessive hemorrhaging you just suffered was merely a flesh wound. In making a getaway, rather than becoming nervous you are able to think instead that smoke is your shadow and that your presence is unimportant and undetectable.

Hypnotization

A Ninja avoids letting his very participation in existence being known, especially when the mission encourages interaction with strangers. Yet, there are times when efficiency demands that he extract the information from an individual where planning, guile, or murder seem contrived. In the unlikely event that a Ninja was compromised during his acts of espionage, he still walks away from the incident and finishes the mission as if it never happened. The guard or civilian who discovered the Ninja simply does not remember having ever spoken to anyone suspicious that afternoon or evening, much less a dark-clothed assassin. Pop culture has somehow come up with the answer to this by instilling the myth that Ninjas could hypnotize their victims, and control their will. In a sense, mind-control and persuasion achieve the same effect in the dark Dao. In the Ninja's case, he is simply implementing skilled rhetoric and a high display of emotional intelligence. He appeals to the common man's vanity by complimenting his clothing. He sates their greed with promises of bribery. He can fool their lusts by dressing and acting as a woman. He can paralyze the cowardly and guilty with threats. He exploits their idleness and baseness of mind by exclaiming a distraction, then suddenly babbling about nothing. Using his understanding of people, a Ninja can cut through people with nothing more than his tongue and mannerisms like a knife through tofu in order to achieve his objective faster.

Resisting Ninja "hypnosis," therefore, is a combination of really knowing yourself and being skilled in the same avenues of rhetoric and persuasion. Know what tempts and can lure you, and be familiar with the techniques to win and capture the hearts and minds of mortals who share your desires or fears. If you can tell when you are being used, and are adept at masking your intent in return, by some high level play you can misguide the Ninja with the information that he thinks he wants but which you know as false.

Meditation

There are entire volumes written on cultivating chi for you to study. Know that the myriad of wonders and skills involved in Meditation does not fall in the realm of expertise for this book. Remember that with the practice and study of meditation you are still training. But unlike the building up of other skills, your education and mastery can be reached to completion by yourself, alone. No partners, competition, or tools are necessary.

A general consensus is to have a strong back and a soft front. The spine is erect and straight rather than slouched; legs ideally crossed in lotus sutra position (though if this is not possible, a half lotus is acceptable to gradually train the flexibility of the ankles and knees). Every muscle in the body needs to relax, so the face must not be tensed (no furrowing of eyebrows or grinding of the jaw). Press the tongue gently to the roof of the mouth. If there is pain anywhere in the body adjust posture or identify any tenseness and soothe the ailing site through breathing. Eyelids should droop calmly over your pupils, which, if open, are never looking above "eye level" and about 45 degrees towards the ground. Focus on your breath.

The heart is trained to intake more oxygen through aerobic and cardio-intensive training, as well as the seemingly mundane performance of inhaling and exhaling. While few humans can stop involuntary muscle actions such as one's own heartbeat, learning to master a deceptively insignificant motor function performed daily is of great importance to truth-seekers and the modern warrior. Multiple objectives exist to clear the mind, heal the body, alter the soul, encounter different planes, achieve enlightenment or disappear. Even while facing against a mortal nemesis the master's breathing remains ever steady— he parts with his breath steadily, using bursts of breath for quick attacks sparingly. In daily conduct, he learned how to disguise and stifle his chi to avoid detection. Highly attuned, he has also learned how to sense other people's chi.

Misconceptions plague the art of meditation as ubiquitous as myths float around about Ninja. It is not necessary to empty your mind completely, or to forcefully banish thoughts. You do not need to "see" nothing but the forced blackness of your eyelids (for example, visualizing certain colors or Kanji characters may work). Nor are you aiming to annihilate the ego. The presence of the mind need not limit itself to stilling, healing or affecting only yourself, but may also extend to bestow its effect upon the room of the enlightened and nearby vicinity, if not the world. The monks who pray upon the peak have their collective efforts affect the whole of the mountain, thereby transforming and enabling its tranquillity.

Below are more self-training ideas for meditation, all unconventional and unorthodox in their approach.

> *"He who conquers others is powerful. He who*
> *conquers/controls himself is mighty"*
> *- Chapter XXXIII, Dao De Jing*

Attack and defend with individual hands. The goal is to separate the minds of the individual limbs. The trick lies in positioning the angle of one hand to direct punches towards your face/heart/or solar plexus while maintaining a realistic blocking/parrying one for your defending hand. Avoid grabbing, and if you have to "trap" with the defending hand, make sure the thumb is aligned with the other fingers rather than sticking out on its own. Alternate the roles of left and right hands as offense and defense. For proper training, keep the upper body occupied while in rigid horse stance and switching between frontal and cat stances according to the attacking punch. Experiment with different strikes (see the "Combat" section), while limiting the blocks and parries to less than a few variations. See if you can memorize any certain combos.

Training while Sitting Down (Dodging)

The necessities of life may demand you to be sitting down behind a desk or in a car on the daily drive to work, often for hours. These sedentary breaks, pauses at red lights or traffic— need not be fruitless training-wise. These are opportunities to practice every martial movement pertaining from the waist above. While no one is looking, practice head-movement in boxing, simultaneous blocking/punching from Wing Chun, etc. Several South-Asian martial arts such as Indonesian Penchak Silat train beginning parrying and receiving punch drills with partners facing across from each other sitting with legs criss-crossed. With this in mind, you may practice the attacking and defending oneself while sitting down. Practice dodging projectiles thrown at you, ducking or moving spine first, followed by shoulders and the head to the other side.

Controlled Circular Defending

Instead of attacking and defending at full speed, conserve your chi and punch and parry as if you were swimming in water. You will prioritize defending over punching and kicking, with less emphasis on tight, perfect technique. Instead, your movements over-extend and telegraph in full range of motion, lubricating the joints and stimulating blood flow. Visualize the punches coming towards and parry with wide, circular movements, almost "feeling" the contact of the punches upon your forearms through projection of chi. Though footwork is slow, it is controlled and solidly grounded. If you were to pause mid-movement you would not be caught off balance.

Self-template

Begin at the lowest level stripping the weapon from the wielding hand in a coordination exercise or a variation of the attacking and defending from oneself. With a solid grip on the weapon, begin tracing or staking valid targets on your own body without making contact. Knives must have fluid movements and immediately follow stabs with slashes, and palm-sticks or kubatons and any other blunt-tipped object must strike important nerves, trapping the limbs and leaping unto the throat, for example. Because you are using a trainer weapon, feel the coldness of the aluminum training knife against your flesh, being ever aware of the damage a real one of steel can do against your muscle and tissue. You are training yourself to learn the vulnerable targets of the body to attack, and in doing so train sensitivity to having yours being struck in the future.

Buddhism as the Enemy

In some languages, to forsake one's career, abandon material possessions, and choosing to follow the path of Buddha is called: "exiting the family." It is a mistake to think exiting the world and embracing reclusiveness is an escape from the Ninja. Something other than karma ties two souls together in a contract. If you have an appointment with the Ninja he would hound you to the ends of the Earth. All of Japanese bushido is inextricably tied to Buddhism. It is difficult to picture the serene face of Buddha, closed eyelids, long-eared (and big-bellied in some cultures) as an adversary. Yet, the benevolent man formed the basis for the religion and philosophy which the Ninja, and all of Japan, stood upon for centuries since its very introduction to the islands. When forming a long term spiritual battle plan against the Ninja, it is essentially recognizing that you are pitting your religion (or lack of it) against his.

This is why you must apply your knowledge of the arts of war to Buddha himself. Begin by knowing the enemy. Read on Buddhism's history, about its many diverting sects, from Chan Buddhism to the Japanese Zen practiced by the Ninjas. Familiarize yourself with its core beliefs, the 8 noble truths, famous parables and tales of the mortal Siddhartha, etc. Who are the famous figureheads and entities in religious Buddhism? What differences are there between Zen and its ancestor, Chinese Chan Buddhism? Then study and begin breaking down its weaknesses. On what concepts do the different sects differ in belief? What were the past criticisms of Buddhism made by its rivals Confucianism and Daoism? Where exactly are its ideological chinks— where the seams of logic appear to come apart? One critical piece of knowledge is the glaring paradox of murder contrasting with the benevolent mantra of Buddha to not kill. How can you use the concept of karma against the Ninja, ideally before weapons are drawn?

Many esoteric practices and "spells" of the Ninja such as its intricate hand-signs known as *Kuji-kiri* or *Kuji-in* are influenced by Buddhist principles (and some Daoist ones, possibly). Understand the ideological mechanisms as well as the science behind suggestiveness in psychology for these methods and you will be a step closer to ensuring your triumph and survival against the Ninja.

Daoism stresses action and immortality. Buddhism is ephemeral and relies on waiting, chanting of mantras, etc. As a Daoist, you do not believe in karma. You are responsible for paving the path to your own fate.

Strategies

In preparing for their dark education Ninjas did not put a premium on techniques, so much as they did upon strategy. In fact, it is believed that historical Ninja derived much of their tactics from Chinese war manuals from which their Japanese ancestors likely derived from. This is why you are encouraged in "Acquisition of Knowledge" to obtain what tomes you can and read and consume knowledge as abundantly as possible. Read Western classics (*Leviathan* by Hobbes, *The Prince* by Machiavelli, etc.) and Eastern classics (any numerous philosophy books to martial ones such as the aptly-written Daoist texts *Art of War* and *I*

Ching, etc.) to suit the operation appropriate to your current hemisphere. Understand the origins and history behind a people's thinking and way of life.

For your convenience and reading pleasure, below are a list of possible strategies to encountering and dealing with a particular Ninja, each with their unique mindset, approaches and weapons of choice.

Giaour Strategy

If the Ninja is of Japanese descent almost 90% of the time his target may have to resort to the strategy of an outsider. Aware that he is facing an enemy with alien paradigms and culture, he therefore finds solace and strength in his own. He capitalizes on the specific strengths, legends and myth associated with his particular ethnicity/people's way of life and evokes them before and during the encounter. With luck he will find just the right combination of superstition and bluff to instill barbarian disgust or fear in his enemy, giving him the advantage.

With the rise of globalization so many have become like floating driftwood and inexplicably depressed, unaware that their loss of "self" is tied to becoming culturally rootless from their ancestors. This is why you must become grounded in your culture. Remember, the Ninja is counting on your lack of filial piety and alienation. Imitations of perfection are pathetic. Do not be fooled for a second that you can somehow best the Ninja at what he does. He *wants* you to be seduced by his culture, for you to partake in the illusion hearkening back to a time and land so alien and hostile that it is impossible to comprehend even for modern day Japanese. Would a proud Viking descendant abandon his surname to learn diluted fake "Karate" and start imitating Japanese diction and mannerisms?

Zhu Ge Liang Strategy

The most learned of the strategies would much rather be seen directing those physically stronger and more skilled than him to deal with threats than engaging in it directly himself. His emotional intelligence; persuasion; charisma and overall likeability means that he has many loyal friends willing to back him up and gang up on the assailant when necessary. He excels in all matters of intel-gathering and deception as exalted in the Art of War, and would find out the price of the contract, and if it is high enough, somehow exploit and play any competing ninjas' greed against each other. Being a man of logic, he finds no moral qualms with possessing and using numbers against an enemy, even if it is just one lone individual since he knows it can mean his life on the line.

Never let it be said that this book does not encourage one to make friends. Friends are currency, by which its amassing and spending stalls defeat and even death. He understands that while friends can betray, they can also lead to connections that allow for quick success or eventual victory.

Bushido Strategy

While it is said that samurai are the "enemy" of ninjas in the same conviction said of cats and dogs, the historical Ninja avoided confronting a samurai or any armed warrior in fair combat in the open at all costs. The swordsman trained in the warrior arts of Bushido expected to survive based off his superior knowledge and instincts of the martial art. While the Ninja disregards honor, nobility and mercy as useless, the Bushido turns inwards during his meditations and exploits them as the very qualities of strength which the Ninja lack.

Shaolin Strategy

At the core of his strength is his faith, which, if shaken may prove to be fatal against the Ninja. All his body-hardening, gruesome calisthenics-honed kung fu and tortured muscles are accessories to the soul encased in the flesh. Since the historical Ninja was almost definitely Buddhist, they may even arrive to a temporary truce given the right circumstances and words of the Monk. A miracle may be achieved in converting the Ninja through his piousness and staying true to his enlightened image and actions.

Beggar Strategy

Mystique and sublime awe surrounds the organized beggar community, varying in respect throughout the ages and different cultures. Unrestrained by any material obligations and rapacious ambition, survival has and always will be the beggar's top skill being cultivated since his inception into the world of rags and humility.

He relies on improvisation where he lacks in wherewithal. When cornered he may unleash the wrath of an animal, betraying his brutal years scumming and scrapping amidst the lowest of the low. He is familiar with dirty fighting and like the tactician, finds nothing wrong with ganging up as seven men on one enemy, especially if the one man was Ninja.

A dog has always been considered the enemy of beggars. However, historically Ninja have arguably feared the dog even worse, since the keen nose and sensitivity of the canine to life signs of intruders has always made his missions more difficult. When dangers get too thick, the beggar escapes through disguise and the heavy cloaking of strangers or into the herd of other fellow beggars.

A small favor...

Thank you for purchasing and reading *How to Beat a Ninja*. No doubt after reading and thoroughly digesting its contents you are motivated; have become more knowledgeable and prepared than the average layman on facing the Ninja threat, and will return to reread your copy many times more.

Before you depart, please do me the small favor of taking a few minutes to write a few lines about this book on Amazon. Every single review will be read and taken into account for future revisions and titles.

About the Author

Wu Song is a traveller, writer, and martial artist who holds Black belts and championships in several styles and sports, both Eastern and Occidental. He has survived an encounter with a Ninja twice.

www.ingramcontent.com/pod-product-compliance
Lightning Source LLC
Chambersburg PA
CBHW051832040426
42447CB00006B/494